The College Life
Survival Guide
for Girls

Legal & Disclaimer

The information contained in this book and its contents is not designed to replace or take the place of any form of medical or professional advice; and is not meant to replace the need for independent medical, financial, legal, or other professional advice or services, as may be required. The content and information in this book have been provided for educational purposes only.

The content and information contained in this book have been compiled from sources deemed reliable, and it is accurate to the best of the Author's knowledge, information, and belief. However, the author cannot guarantee its accuracy and validity and cannot be held liable for any errors and/or omissions. Further, changes are periodically made to this book as and when needed. Where appropriate and/or necessary, you must consult a professional (including but not limited to your doctor, attorney, financial advisor, or such other professional advisor) before using any of the suggested remedies, techniques, or information in this book.

Table of contents

Introduction

Congratulations, you're going to college! The big question is, now what? Maybe you're feeling a bit anxious about how you'll survive on your own, away from your family? Or maybe you're looking for the best advice to be successful and happy in college?

Transitioning to college is a challenge for all students. The transition marks an essential milestone in growing up from teenager to adulthood. This significant step can be both exciting and challenging for you and your family. Moving away to college can be both a scary and amazing experience in a girl's life. The fact is though that your time in college can be one of the best times of your life.

You will be moving away from familiar places and people to a new life filled with new experiences and new people. You will be leaving your childhood behind and taking the first steps in becoming an adult. When you start to think about learning to manage on your own, it can seem like a massive task and like any life change, can cause anxiety as we adapt to our new life.

Some women find the college experience a real struggle, but the good news is that it doesn't have to be! It's no secret that for some students college is a bit of a survival challenge, particularly at first, and this should be recognised. You're in a new city, you don't know many people, your toilet is blocked, your fridge is empty and your exams are looming!

Don't panic! This book is full of advice, hints and tips to help you to prepare and succeed in college. We will share practical tips to help new female college students and soon-to-be female college students to survive and thrive in college. With the proven tips and strategies in this book you'll be able to enjoy the college experience to the full, and come out of college a strong, independent woman, ready for the adult world.

Changes that college will bring

Going away to college is a big change for anyone, but how difficult it is depends on the individual. Moving away from home can be a real challenge for some people because they may not know anyone who is going to the same college. They are leaving school friends behind, and are worried about finding new buddies.

Everyone has a unique experience of leaving home to go to college hours, but college girls often fail to recognize how many of them face the same challenges. Almost everyone is leaving home, everyone is getting used to a new learning environment, everyone is looking to meet new friends.

One of the most challenging aspects of attending college is that so much is unknown. You probably don't know who your roommates will be, what it's like to use a communal bathroom, or what the college workload will be. Most people, even the ones who seem confident, will be feeling unsure about how to live so far away from their home and their friends.

As you stand in line to get your room keys, or wave your parents goodbye after they've dropped off your luggage, the sadness can hit like a brick wall. As you turn your head around to see if you know anyone from the crowd and don't recognize even one, the feeling of anxiety can make you wonder if you made the right decision to make the move.

Maybe you didn't want to leave home because it meant being separated from your family and best friends. You might be leaving activities and clubs behind. You might miss your pets.

On the other hand, you might be eager to get to college, say goodbye to all the rules and regulations you're used to at home and finally enjoy some more freedom.

Whatever your background you may find it difficult to adjust because, at least at first, living outside of your comfort zone can be a challenging experience. The thing to remember in all of this is that college can become your new home, your friends become your new family and you can find new interests.

College can be exciting and challenging at the same time. You can create a ton of memories with new college friends you'll have for life, but on the other hand, professors might swamp you with piles of paperwork – assignments, projects, homework, term papers and case studies that you have to get done on time also.

Whether you intend to live on campus or not, many aspects of your life will change. You will have opportunities to meet new people. You will have more independence and freedom and new responsibilities. College life also brings challenges that can feel overwhelming - but they don't have to be!

Homesickness and loneliness are common experiences, especially for first-year students in college. You may cry over the phone the first time your parents reach out to you, or you may not. None of this is unusual. Don't be embarrassed by whatever emotions you feel and don't feel you should apologize for them. As you become used to college life, you will realize that this was part of the transition to you becoming independent and learning to handle situations on your own.

If you feel lonely, accept that this isn't a failing and understand that you are not alone. Loneliness is something that most new college girls struggle with from time to time. Accept this, accept that you are not alone. This will pass.

The transition to college life is significant, and we don't always anticipate the most challenging aspects. Parents, friends and family frequently sugar-coat the change, claiming that college will be the best time of your life and more. Hopefully it will be, but initially it can feel strange to move to an entirely new environment with completely new people and be expected to become great friends with the people we live with. It is a significant transition, and it's easy to feel that we should hide and bottle up our struggles when we have difficulty adjusting to a new situation. Nobody has to do that.

Awareness of what awaits you can help lessen the impact of stress and anxiety you will be dealing with when separated from your family and familiar things. In this guide will will help you to prepare, covering a lot of topics including:

- Packing preparation
- Making new friends and managing conflicts
- Fighting homesickness
- Day-to-day survival
- Developing healthy eating habits and fitness routines
- Classroom and study difficulties
- Taking care of your mental health

This is your first big step into adult life as a woman. Did you know that 40% of students drop out of college every year in the USA? Well, that's not going to be you, because this book will share with you the proven tips & strategies to make your college days the best days of your life. So let's get started!

Packing for College

When you are going to live away from home for the first time, thinking of what to bring into your new place can be daunting. Don't panic! Put together a list of what you need and use it as a checklist when gathering things together and packing.

Packing Tips for College

If you are staying in the college dorm, expect that you will be sharing your room with someone you haven't met before. You may have a long list of things you want to bring with you, but remember that you won't have a huge space and you can't take the whole house with you!

When thinking of things to include in your list, think of the essentials – only those things you can't live without. Here are some of these:

- Clothes, underwear, shoes, coat
- Sports clothes
- Phone, computer, backup storage, chargers
- Alarm clock, college books,
- Small medical kit
- Bath and toilet essentials

Get a pen and paper, start a list on your phone or open up a blank document on your laptop - whatever works for you get on to that list. Break it down into categories depending on your needs.

Here is an example:

Clothes

When packing clothes, you have to consider the weather conditions depending on the location of the college you are attending. Will you need warm clothes for the winter, or lighter summer clothes? Is your college in a location that gets four seasons in one day?!.

- Shirts – tees, sweatshirts, jackets, cardigans
- Pants – casual, workout, slacks, denim, cozy pants.
- Undergarments – panties, bras

- Nightwear – pajamas or lingerie
- Protective gear – hats, mittens, boots, umbrella
- Shoes – sneakers or running shoes, sandals, and a pair of heels for special occasions
- Belts and bags
- Shorts
- Bathrobes
- House slippers
- Coats - light or heavy

Bedding

- Comforter
- Bed Sheets
- Pillow and Pillow covers
- Duvet

Home and Kitchen Gadgets

- Coffee maker
- Electric kettle
- Mug and cup
- Plates, bowls,
- Rice cooker
- Chopping board
- Condiments organizers

- Drinking glasses
- Plastic food storage
- Eating utensils (2-3 sets)
- Can opener

Home and Laundry Essentials

- Laundry bag
- Laundry detergent
- Stain remover
- Fabric softener
- Disinfectants
- Dishwashing liquid
- Sponges
- Rubber gloves

Toilet, Bath, and Personal Care Essentials

- Soap – facial and body soaps
- Shampoo and conditioner
- Loofah
- Body wash and bath salts
- Body towels
- Shaving cream
- Razors

- Shower shoes
- Moisturizers and facial cleansers
- Toothbrush and toothpaste
- Mouthwash and dental floss
- Sanitary products
- Deodorants
- Nail clippers
- Nail file
- Nail polish
- Nail polish remover
- Hairbrush
- Hairspray
- Curling and straightening iron
- Hair ties, clips, ribbons, etc.
- Cotton pads, cotton swabs, or cotton balls
- Makeup and makeup remover
- Body lotion
- Scissors
- Perfume
- Towels
- Sewing kit

Friends

Making new friends can really help your self-esteem, learning, and academic growth. Having meaningful college friendships during your undergraduate or graduate studies will lead to a better social life and a greater feeling of belonging. It can also be the foundation of a successful and fulfilling education, leading to sought-after employment prospects.

Students who make an effort to build friendships in college are more likely to succeed academically and graduate on time. If you are determined to succeed in your studies you might fall into the trap of spending long hours studying but in the process overlooking the need for social interaction. It is important to put time and effort into your studies but don't let the pressure to succeed overwhelm you to the point that you overlook the need to develop friendships and take time out. Taking a balanced approach to down-time is crucial to success.

Making New Friends

Humans are known to be social animals. We create and foster friendships to have someone to rely on, listen to, or to be there for in times of need— this is how we are.

Friendship allows us to understand, empathize with, and nurture one another. With friends, we bring out the best in one another and can be confident of emotional support during trying times, without the fear of being judged. Good friends will be able to support you when college life feels like hard work, and you will be able to do the same for them.

Studies reveal that college participants who built a close social circle gain social support and academic motivation. These students performed well by studying together, de-stressing regularly, supporting each other in their academic feats, and celebrating their success.

Meanwhile, a lack of friendship and social contact can generate feelings of loneliness, emptiness, and isolation that gradually chip away at emotional well-being.

Of course, building new connections in a melting pot of students from diverse backgrounds and circumstances can be super challenging. While there will be same-age learners like you who start college straight out of high school, there will also be more mature individuals who may be restarting their college life after raising a family or maybe others taking a new career path. These factors, plus the reality that you're still finding your way in a new environment and trying to integrate into new classroom and campus cultures, may at first make it feel hard to make connections.

So, what measures can you use to gain meaningful and powerful connections with good friends during your college years?

In Class

As a rule of the thumb, remember this: You can make more friends by showing interest in other people than by expecting them to be interested in you. If you show that you want to know more about people they will start to open up to you, and then they will want to know more about you.

If building a social network is quite a challenge for you, remember that others at your college or university face the same dilemma as you. They are looking for opportunities to make friends as well.

Whatever new situation you are in, introduce yourself, people will appreciate your effort to reach out to them. A casual conversation with them will help you discover common connections that may start a lifetime of adventure and memorable experiences.

Some classes offer better opportunities to broaden your inner circle. For instance, classes that encourage group activities or projects, no matter how offputting they may feel sometimes, create greater chances for classmates to communicate and build connections. After all, they have more time to talk with each other during these times compared to those classes with straight-up lectures.

On-Campus

Campus events are an incredible way to meet new people. They provide a topic that invites discussion or presents different perspectives (particularly events with guest speakers) and cater to introverts and extroverts alike. Many of these gatherings have a reception before or after. These occasions present attractive opportunities to strike up a conversation.

Thanks to the various social media platforms it's easy to find out what is going on, so engage in social media and on-line notice boards. As you move around campus keep your eyes open for events advertised old-style on posters. You'll probably feel spoiled for choice, as there's probably something going on every night of the week.

Also think about where you might meet new people:

The student center (or the student commons): The building is primarily devoted to student recreation and socialization. Since it often holds student activities, it's a nice place to initiate a casual conversation.

At the gym: If you're working out, you can easily find individuals with a shared interest and start your friendship.

The hall: Waiting in the hall is an open opportunity to meet people who interest you or are interested in you.

Around campus: You might even start up a conversation with someone heading in the same direction as you. If you are shy this might feel like something you'd never do, but you might be surprised at the effect just a smile in someone's direction can have.

In the dormitory: You're likely to spend a lot of time in your dorm, especially during your first year. Dorms are usually packed with students who, like you, are both excited and a little bit scared. They are an excellent venue for spontaneous interaction. Whether you're simply hanging out in the common area doing your assignments, brushing your teeth in the communal bathroom, or doing something fun in the hallway, it doesn't matter, these people are potentially your friends.

If you have roommates, you might want to go together to knock on neighbors' doors to see if they would like to get together. Bringing some snacks or sweets will help you make a good impression. Remember to attend the events hosted by your Resident Assistant. Such informal gatherings are designed to bring your floor's occupants together in a comfortable setting to nurture new relationships.

The above applies to other living conditions (for example, sharing a house or apartment unit with other folks). Even if you live outside the campus, you should always prioritize getting to know your neighbors and room-mates.

Avoiding People

We're not going to dwell on this too much, but it's worth saying that you are perfectly entitled to avoid people who you don't feel comfortable around or who you just don't get on with. It's a fact of life that we won't get on with everyone and that's OK. You can be civil and polite to someone without needing to form a friendship.

Dealing with Conflict

Conflict is unavoidable in life. It can range from simply disagreeing with someone to a full-fledged, long-running feud. As a college student, experiencing conflict is quite normal. After all, a college or a university campus is a common ground for diverse perspectives, values, and beliefs. Sometimes women can lack confidence in standing their ground in these situations. Often men are more vocal and forceful when dealing with conflict.

To handle conflict, here are some valuable suggestions to give you some strategies to consider:

Be accommodating. You might not win an argument, but you can win a friend. This simple (although challenging) decision can protect the peace and be helpful in certain situations. Just be aware that you don't have to be accommodating all the time, your point of view is as important as anyone else's.

Ignore the issue. It might sound counter-intuitive, but it works in some situations, especially ones that aren't worth the effort or critical enough to waste your time and energy on. This approach allows both parties more time to develop a more appropriate solution to address the problem. Sometimes the problem just goes away.

Allow compromises. We have learned this method since we were kids. This approach satisfies both parties as each party must give up something from their side. It reduces tension and stress and serves as an excellent first step for people who aren't yet familiar with each other. Think about what small thing you could compromise on that would satisfy the other party. Consider what they might be able to bend on that would make you feel better as well.

Compete for a resolution. Someone will lose in this zero-sum game, but you must refuse to compromise and insist on resolving the problem. This method is necessary from time to time, mainly when you need to implement a quick solution to an issue. In this situation, you must prioritize what needs to be done over your future relationship with the other party. There is a strategy called The Broken Record Technique that can be very effective in situations where you cannot compromise or change your mind. You can Google for more information on this.

Collaborate to come up with a solution. This approach requires more time, effort, and commitment to resolve an issue. It also necessitates a certain level of trust, allowing both parties to believe that they have a share in the outcome and foster a long-term relationship. Of course, both parties have shared responsibilities for whatever result there might be. In case you need immediate action to resolve a conflict, these suggestions will help you achieve your objective:

- Allow yourself to cool down first to think more carefully about what you need to say and do.
- Discuss it calmly with the other person. They too are presumably looking for a solution.
- Determine the points you can agree on and make this a starting point.

- Rather than focusing on personality, pay attention to behavior and events (for example, "It seems to me that you sometimes leave things disorganized." instead of "You're such a slacker!").
- Always actively listen to the other person's point of view.
- Determine the source of the conflict and ensure that it doesn't get out of hand.
- Create a list of the most critical issues. If you disagree on numerous points, pick one to focus on right now.
- Come up with solutions together. Exert effort to be inventive and experiment with new ideas.
- Always remain respectful and upbeat. Believe in your ability to discover a solution.
- Seek assistance from someone unbiased like your RA, academic advisor or trusted friend.

What to Do When You're Shy

If you're worried about going to college as a shy girl who wants to make more friends, these ideas will help you achieve your goal. It may take some time, but you will eventually find your pals. You could set yourself a goal to do one small thing every day to practise making contact with others.

Find Places and People with Similar Interests

One of the best starting points is to look for opportunities to find people who share your hobbies, interests, and values. Like-minded people attract each other, and because you have a common ground, you will understand each other better and may even create a solid bond to last a lifetime.

Where do you find these potential friends?

Faith-based services and locations: These offer students opportunities for spiritual growth and development through activities, events, and counseling. Many campuses provide multi-faith spaces that cater to students who identify with any religious group. These are also open to those who are spiritual but not religious.

You can also look for opportunities to meet with others of the same faith. By attending church or temple, maybe faith study groups. Since you share the same beliefs and faith, this will increase the likelihood of you finding people you can bond with.

Small sports groups: If you're the type who likes to stay fit, joining a small sports group will help you accomplish two or more of your goals; making friends and keeping your body in shape. A smaller group will feel less daunting because you will only meet a few new people at a time.

Small activity groups: Whether it may be theater and the arts, media and publication, cultural, or the debate club, joining activity groups can introduce you to connections and friendships that go beyond shared interests or passions. As with the small sports groups, you will meet a small number of people at a time.

What to Do If You're Lonely

Finally, dealing with loneliness is a common aspect of college life. If you are lonely, you must take action before you start to feel too bad. As suggested above, you could join a club, a sports team, or a religious organization and participate in their activities. You can attend events hosted by the university. Invite folks to join you for coffee or study sessions. Getting yourself busy will help you avoid feeling lonely.

Sometimes taking active steps can be hard. If that happens be aware that you can reach out to organizations found on the Internet who can offer support. The Verywellfamily website is just one source of advice, the MIND site is also a great resource.

If you have depression or anxiety, don't hesitate to seek help. There's nothing to be ashamed of about what you're going through. With the proper mental health treatment, you'll be able to cope and feel better in no time.

Dealing with Homesickness

Your newfound freedom has a cost, and that's leaving the comforts of your childhood home. The feeling of homesickness happens during transition periods and even after those times. It's akin to the feelings of grief and loss which can occur to anybody, whatever age and in many situations. These feelings don't make you weak, immature, stupid, or abnormal.

It's only natural to miss home, especially during the holidays or winter break. If you're struggling with homesickness, below are some suggestions on how you can generate a sense of home on campus:

- Acknowledge your feeling of homesickness and understand that it is normal and it isn't permanent.
- Set your goals and expectations for your college life.
- Make yourself at home on campus by getting to know your new surroundings.
- Personalize your space with pictures from home.
- Establish daily routines that will help you remove your focus on negative feelings.
- Set new habits that will make your new environment feel like home.

- Seek opportunities to build your social network on campus.
- Participate in community service programs as a volunteer.
- Look for a spiritual or religious group.
- Maintain communication with family and friends. Reach out to them for support and let them know how you feel.

Finding people with whom you can connect and develop a sense of belonging is crucial in college. One of the most incredible things about experiencing college life is the opportunity to be a part of something bigger than yourself.

Dealing with Roommates

Living with a new person can be an excellent way to branch out of your comfort zone and meet new people. It could also be a massive challenge for you because adjusting to something new requires spending energy. Sharing space can be interesting to say the least. You might find your roommate getting on your nerves from time to time. On the flip side, your newfound relationship may lead to a beautiful friendship that lasts a very long time.

When you feel uncertain about how to handle this new shared setup, below are some suggestions for sharing a room:

Get acquainted with your roomie. It is the first and most important rule in living with someone. Find out the basics, such as what interests and irks them, as well as what their boundaries are. Naturally, you won't be "besties" in an instant, but remember that this person will spend a lot of time with you, so it's only wise and fair to get to know them.

Communicate. Communication is vital in any relationship. Tell your roommate everything they should know about you and your suggestions about your setup. Take this opportunity to set your boundaries and talk about your shared responsibilities. It is also preferable to tell them if anything is bothering you before it transforms into a full-blown argument. Bear in mind that things might not all go according to your plans, when you're sharing a room compromise is usually necessary.

Familiarize yourself with each other's schedules. Their timetable determines many things that may affect both of your performances. Let's say you are a night owl and the other person is an early bird. Your nightly activities might disturb them, just as their morning movement sounds could interrupt your sleep. Sit down and talk about this and work out how you can both make things easier for each other. Bear in mind that if you know your roomie's routine you will quickly notice if something seems wrong, for example if they don't come home one night when they planned to. They will be able to do the same for you.

Be respectful. Part of being respectful is being considerate and open-minded. Your roommate may come from a different background or culture, which may mean that they have different values. Your habits and personalities might well be different, but try to meet in the middle to avoid conflict. For instance, always check with your roommate when you want to invite friends over or when you need to do something that might disturb them. Always ask their permission when you want to borrow something.

Invest in headphones. Your headphones don't merely deter unwanted interruptions but they can also help maintain silence and peace in your room. While you and your roomie may share the same taste in music, movies, or TV series, that doesn't permit you to blast the volume of whatever you're watching or listening to for them to hear. Wear your headphones whenever you go sound-tripping or binge-watching.

Be nice. Even if your new roommate isn't the most amiable person you've ever met or you have contrasting personalities, play it nice. The mood in the room and your interaction with them can significantly impact your new lifestyle and academic performance.

Give them some breathing space. Personal space can become a significant concern with roommates. Transitioning into a smaller living area can be inconvenient, and sharing your place with another person can make it even more challenging. Leave your roommate a few hours in the room to themselves each week, and they will hopefully reciprocate.

Sororities

A sorority is a college campus organization whose goal is to build a sense of camaraderie and community, among other things. Women join a sorority, whereas men join a fraternity.

Each sorority group has its own goals, rules, and expectations. You can join a sorority if you demonstrate that you possess the qualities that meet their specific requirements. The attributes they are looking for are usually based on your personality, academic achievements, community involvement, and campus engagement. The process of recruiting sorority members is called a rush. During the process of getting to know sorority members the potential recruits are called rushees. Bear in mind that sorority sisters will vote at the end of the process to decide which rushees can join them, so nothing is a done deal. Don't on any account be demoralized if you don't end up in your first choice sorority, it doesn't change who you are.

Many first-year college students want to join a sorority or fraternity because it creates a sense of social integration and enables them to build relationships and friendships, however it's not an essential part of college life.

What are the benefits of joining a sorority?

Academics

Most sororities set a minimum GPA requirement, encouraging you to focus on your studies and perform well in your coursework. If your GPA goes too low after you've been initiated, the sorority will place you under probation.

But it isn't all doom and gloom. Sororities encourage sisters to learn together. Hence, study groups and rooms are frequently rented exclusively for sorority sisters.

Campus Involvement and Influence

You'll learn to be a leader on campus, a skill that will also come in handy in your future profession.

Sorority and fraternity members actively participate in many organizations, such as the student government, student affairs, and other student-led societies. Participating in extracurricular activities can help you improve your curriculum vitae for job applications, summer employment, and internships after graduation.

Charitable Endeavors

Many sororities are involved in philanthropy and charity works. As a result, you'll be expected to participate in these events and get more interested in charity.

You may be required to not only participate in these activities as a member of a sorority but also to organize them. Members frequently assist in registering people for various charitable organizations, planning fundraising events, and managing the "Philanthropy Day" for the sorority.

Social and Professional Connections

Joining a sorority is also one of the most effective methods to broaden your career options. Active alumni of your sorority who are frequently recruiting prefer sisters from their sorority group, so staying active in your sorority after college is a good option.

You'll have a lifelong social network, friends with whom you share deep personal connections, and professional benefits. These are vital relationships since your sorority sisters will always be there to support, encourage, and celebrate with you.

Hazing and initiation

You will be aware that in the past, particularly in fraternities, there have been some pretty awful hazing and initiation rituals. To a certain extent this happened in some sororities as well. These rituals were humiliating and sometimes dangerous and colleges have taken action to stop them now. This means that you are very unlikely to be subjected to anything similar if you pledge to join a sorority. However, in the event that you find yourself in any situation where you do not feel comfortable - be strong and walk away. In all of your time in college only take part in things that you want to, and that you feel comfortable with.

Drink, Drugs, Dating and going out

You should be able to look back on college as a time when you were able to enjoy a new-found freedom, build friendships and maybe a special relationship. It's a fantastic time to be young and filled with energy and ideas. However it would be wrong to avoid mentioning some of the pitfalls that you may encounter.

Drink

We tend not to think of alcohol as a drug but of course it can be just as much of a problem as anything else. It can be addictive, it can make us lose control of our actions and can compromise our health.

Firstly, the legal age to drink will depend on what country you live in. For some it's 18 years of age. For others, it's 21 years of age. Being realistic, there aren't many college students who don't get carried away a little in the excitement of a good party. It would be great if the following massive hangovers would put them off repeating the performance, but that is generally not the case. Take responsibility for yourself, and stay strong. If you decide to drink alcohol, be moderate and stop as soon as you start to feel the effects. You went to college for a reason, which is to study and get the qualifications you need to set you up for the rest of your life. Don't compromise that for the sake of getting drunk. You need to be bright and ready to work in the mornings, not fighting a hangover and feeling queasy (or worse!). Remember that regular misuse of alcohol can lead to alcoholism, a terrible addiction, and can damage your body.

Whatever you drink when you are out there is a safety issue that all girls need to be aware of. That is that sometimes drinks get spiked. Rohypnol and GHB are two of the most common "date rape" drugs. If you are unfortunate enough to drink these down you will quickly start to lose control of your body and become disorientated. So keep your drink with you. If you need to go to the lavatory, have a friend keep your drink with them. If you realize that you have left your drink for a while maybe it's safer to just abandon it and go get another. It's sad that we have to think this way, but we do.

Drugs

We could write pages on the dangers of drugs to try to persuade new college students to avoid drugs, but the message is simple - just don't. Don't risk your health, your studies and your personal safety for any sort of high.

Drugs can be dangerous in their own right, and they are sometimes contaminated. Drugs can and do kill students every year. It's just not worth it.

It's almost certain that at some time in your college career you will be offered drugs. Be aware that this doesn't always happen in a social setting, students use drugs to help themselves to stay awake for studying, and to help them to sleep. If you do your best to have a healthy lifestyle, if you plan your timetable to study sensibly, you don't need drugs to get through college. When you're out socializing you can have a great time without taking anything to try to enhance your mood.

Be the strong one who stays in control of life without relying on mind-altering plants or chemicals.

Dating

Most students will date while they are in college and go through all the emotional highs and lows that come with that. It can be a great distraction from studies but we're only human and just have to work our way through it! Here are some things you might want to bear in mind:

Most guys are good guys and just as nervous and uncertain about dating someone new as we are. There are some bad apples out there though, so be ready for that. This advice applies if your date is female as well of course.

Until you get to know your date a bit better, tell a friend where you are going and who you are going with. Have an arrangement to ring them at a certain time to confirm you are back in your room and a plan to contact them if you aren't. Be reliable about this, if you're running late make sure your friend knows. If you don't follow the arrangements they will stop bothering to check.

For first dates, meet in a public place. If you feel that you don't want to take things any further, be polite and don't be afraid to leave.

On the other hand, if you think things are going great you might want to still avoid going off to a more private place, decline any invitations to go back to the guy's room. Expect to be respected. There's no need to rush anything.

If you get to a more intimate stage in your relationship this might sound obvious - but when the time comes use a barrier form of protection and consider using secondary birth control such as the pill as well. Getting pregnant isn't the only thing that can go wrong. There are a variety of sexually transmitted infections and diseases that can be caught. Heterosexual people can and still do catch HIV.

Depending on your chosen method, you might need consent from a guardian if you are still a minor. It's essential to be aware of the laws where you live.

Consent matters

Never, ever feel that you have to do anything that you are not comfortable with in a relationship. You do not have to try something new to "see if you like it" when you are pretty sure that you won't. Sex should never feel demeaning, it should never make you feel unhappy, it should never leave you in pain. It should be an intimate and joyful sharing between two people.

However much you feel you love someone, if they are trying to persuade you to do something that you don't want to - walk away. If they are trying to force you to do anything - leave immediately.

If someone does something to you against your will, without your consent, it is rape. It doesn't have to be full sex, it can be a sexual act caried out against your will. It is rape even if it happens in what appears to be a loving relationship.

If someone forces themselves on you in any situation, whether it be at a party or in your own room, it is rape. If you were unable to consent because you were under the influence of drink or drugs that doesn't change anything. Whatever the situation you are not to blame, the person who committed the act is.

If you are ever in a situation where you are unfortunate to have suffered a physical or sexual assault please do not keep it to yourself. Seek support from a trusted friend, go straight to an adult in authority and get help.

Pregnancy

Sometimes life takes a turn that you never wanted or expected. If you think that you might be pregnant don't put off taking action, or lay awake at nights wondering if you are - take a test and find out.

If you are pregnant it is very important that you act quickly to get advice and consider your options. There will be challenging times ahead and difficult decisions to be made. Talk to someone you trust, or if you feel more comfortable with someone who doesn't know you at first, speak to your doctor or contact a local, independent pregnancy advice service. If you do not want to continue with a pregnancy then unfortunately you will need to be advised on the legal implications in the state where you live.

Going out

Following on from all of this advice, don't let it worry you too much, just bear it all in mind to make sure that you stay safe and enjoy college life.

Don't go out alone at night on campus or elsewhere. Buddy up with someone for company and safety. Women should feel safe to walk anywhere at any time but we know that sadly there are low-lifes out there who will prey on lone women, so we say take a pragmatic approach.

If you are on a night out on the town, or at a party with friends you need to look out for each other. There needs to be a rule that no girl is ever left behind. Talk about this with your friends so that everyone is on the same page. Bear in mind that if your friend is behaving strangely they could be under the influence of drugs or alcohol and need you to intervene and take them home. If you and your group all do this you will stay safe on your nights out.

Any time you are out and you feel uncomfortable don't be embarrassed to act. If a guy is harassing you ask for help from bar staff or your friends. If you start to feel dizzy and disorientated again, tell someone, let them know that you need help. Don't be led away from your friends and the crowd, speak up if you ever feel you are losing control.

When you're taking a cab just take a moment to look at the car and make sure it's not a private vehicle. It's a good idea to travel with company, but if you are alone there is nothing to stop you taking a photo of the car on your phone and sending it to a friend. A genuine cab driver won't mind and will understand why you feel the need to do that.

Following these tips will help you to enjoy the varied and exciting college social life with your new found friends.

College Life

Maybe you have longed for this for the longest time: **Independence**. However, it is easy to underestimate the responsibilities of living alone. Though it may seem trivial, on top of studying, on and off-campus activities, and other social activities you are going to have to deal with daily chores.

It's likely that at home you did some of the chores and housework but not all of them. It's entirely different when you are living independently since you must do every chore yourself, or with help from a roommate.

You will be responsible for everything - including making your bed, laundry, cooking, organizing, and budgeting, among many other things. Now is when you realize that freedom always comes at a price. So don't wait until it's all too much and you don't know what to tackle first, have plans in place from the start.

Day-to-Day Survival Tips

Consider the following pointers to establish a system that will help you manage your daily routine effortlessly. Set up a timetable of chores to be done and try to stick to it. Include your roommate in your plans if you share.

Bed

In the past, you might have tried every excuse not to make your bed every morning. No matter how trivial it may seem, this task signifies consideration and respect for yourself and your roommate if you have one.

No, you don't have to expend much energy to make your bed Pinterest or Instagram-worthy. Fluffing your pillows and flattening your comforter and bed sheet should be enough.

We spend an average of eight hours every day in bed. During that time we sweat and dead skin cells, dirt, body oils, and other grime accumulate on our sheets and bedding. This can cause allergies, acne, and other skin problems and on top of that, it can't contribute to a restful night's sleep.

Make sure that your bed linens are washed once a week and incorporate this into your plan for chores.

The benefits of making our beds every morning are as simple as having a nice comfortable bed to fall into at night. But a tidy bed is the start of a tidy room. A tidy room gives you an organized and comfortable space to study in without distractions.

If washing your linens once a week or more regularly isn't an option, there are a few things you have to do to extend the duration between washes. For one, take a shower before bedtime to limit the amount of sweat, oil, and grime you bring into bed with you. Remove your makeup (which will also avoid some eye problems). Don't eat anything in bed, and never wear your shoes in bed.

Make sure that your pillows are washable and to keep them soft and fluffy wash them every three to five months.

Comforters and Blankets

Comforters and throw blankets don't need to be frequently washed since they have less contact with your skin. Be extra careful when washing your quilt or blanket. Your method should depend on what material they are made from. Check the wash label and follow the instructions.

Heavier blankets and quilts are best left in the care of Laundromats since commercial-sized machines are specially designed to handle them better.

Electric blankets: Heated blankets are designed to be machine washable but follow the manufacturer's instructions to the letter. Failure to do that can make your electric blanket unsafe.

Dealing with Bed bugs

Unfortunately, bed bugs hitch rides in clothing and suitcases in all parts of the world. This means that, with so many people coming together from all parts of the world, colleges are one of the most common places where bed bug infestations are found. So it's worth us spending some time advising on how to deal with them. The first thing to know about bed bugs is that they don't mean that a place is dirty. Bedbugs travel about on luggage and clothing and are happy to set up home in the best four star hotel or the smallest apartment.

Usually the first sign of bedbugs is that someone will get bitten and blood can be seen on bedding. If in doubt you can Google for pictures of typical bedbug bites. They spread quickly, so you have to deal with them immediately. However, eliminating is no easy feat and you should not attempt it yourself. If you believe your room has bed bugs, it's critical to inform your RA immediately. Do not, by any means, douse your room with toxic sprays or "bombs". Doing this is far more dangerous than bed bug infestation. Your RA will make sure the situation is dealt with properly.

To avoid getting bedbugs in the first place, here are some strategies to follow:

- After you have been on vacation, and before packing for college, vacuum your suitcases and bags.
- Take a large trashbag on holidays and keep your suitcase in it during hotel stays.

- Familiarize yourself with how the signs of bed bugs look and check your furniture and bags regularly, using a flashlight.
- If you see any signs of blood on your sheets immediately check for bedbugs.
- Thoroughly check any second hand furniture, baggage or soft furnishings before bringing them into your accommodation.

As always, you can find more detailed information on the Internet.

Laundry

A lot of students have never done any laundry before going to college. Even if you're used to doing laundry at home, you will find that using a college laundry room is an entirely different experience.

Check out the cost of using the campus washers and dryers. Some are free, some accept quarterly installations, and others accept electronic payment via your campus debit card or a prepaid laundry card. Whatever it is, just make sure you have the correct payment method before you run out of clean clothes. Then plan out your laundry schedule and add it to your chores plan.

Carefully Plan Your Laundry Routine

The worst possible time to do your laundry is when you're in a rush, you don't have anything clean to wear, and there's a long waiting line to use the machines. Although each campus is unique, the best possible times to do your laundry are the weekday afternoons and during major events. Expect laundry rooms to be super busy during the evenings and weekends. Also, take advantage of the college or university app that notifies you when washers are available.

Always Sort Your Laundry

It's easier to sort your laundry before you go to the laundry room than try to do it when you get there and may be limited for space.

Group the items by colors and fibers since you don't want your whites smudged with black and your fabrics to shrink or wrinkle. Sort them into groups of white, light, and dark colors or based on how delicate their fabric is. Having a look at the garment care labels, this will help a lot. Generally your laundry will either be delicate or more robust, dark items and whites.

If you only have a few items for a wash load either save them until you have a full load or hand-wash them.

Remember - if you wash coloured items with light items you might find that the colours have run and ruined your best white shirt! If you wash a lovely woolen jumper on a hot setting it might come out just the right size for a five year old child!

We don't want to be boring about laundry so in brief our advice is - Don't forget to read the laundry labels and do what they say.

Determine the Load

Figuring out how much one laundry load is in a new machine can be tricky, especially if it's your first time doing the laundry in your campus laundry room. To determine the load, fill the washer halfway with soiled clothes without stuffing it. This will serve as a guideline. Then, put the load back to your hamper or laundry basket. The amount of clothes inside the basket is the amount you need to put inside the washer for every load. To avoid forgetting this, you could take a photo of the hamper or basket with the measured load.

Check out your surroundings

People aren't great at keeping laundry rooms clean and tidy. Before you spread out your laundry check the surfaces to make sure there isn't detergent or bleach that may permanently damage your clothes.

Inspect inside the machines as well. Look out for items left inside. If you see that the machine is dirty, the easiest thing is probably to clean it. If you're not sure, notify the laundry room manager about the issue.

Don't Forget to Place Labels

Sometimes things get muddled up in the campus laundry room. Labeling your laundry items, such as your detergent, fabric softener and laundry bags, is a good way to avoid disputes about ownership.

Be Mindful When Using a Dryer

First, never use a dryer without a lint trap or filter. Before starting the dryer, you must also ascertain that the lint trap is clean. In doing so, you'll avoid fires, and your garments will dry more quickly. Many commercial dryers default to run on hot cycles, so make it a point to check out the temperature setting before drying your clothes.

Commercial dryers tend to be larger than household ones. You may be able to fit two loads into one machine. As you load your wet laundry into the machine, give each item a brisk shake to fluff it up. This way, the garment will dry faster and have a lesser possibility of having wrinkles. Double-check everything before starting the machine. Keep in mind that opening and closing the door means losing heat and time.

Tips on Getting Rid of Stains

If you happen to experience a mishap, the following will save you from frustration and losing your favorite clothes:

Sweat, Vomit, and Other Bodily Fluids

You need enzyme laundry detergent and oxygenated non-chlorine bleach. The former breaks down the proteins, making it easier to remove the stain. Wash the garment using the hottest setting recommended for the fabric. If an undesirable odor remains even after washing, rewash the garment with a laundry detergent designed to fight odors.

Blood Stains

Firstly, soak the stained garment in cold water, gently rubbing the part with the stain to remove as much blood as possible. If the water turns reddish, replace it continually until it turns clear. Rinse the garment and apply an enzyme laundry detergent (a stronger one if possible). Let it soak for a while to let the stain remover do its work. If the detergent isn't enough, apply a small amount of oxygenated non-chlorine bleach directly to the spot, but be careful as it may be corrosive to some fabrics (i.e., delicate fabrics such as silk and wool).

Red Wine

Cover the stain with salt since it will absorb the wine's color (you will see that the salt will turn pink). Immerse the garment in cold water with enzyme laundry detergent overnight. If needed, repeat the process until the stain is removed and wash the garment as usual.

Fruit and Fruit Juice

Run cold water over the stained spot to dilute the stain. Directly apply an enzyme laundry detergent to the stain, ensuring it is covered completely. Allow it to soak for around 20 minutes. Do not rinse the detergent; wash the garment at the hottest temperature applicable to its fabric.

Coffee

Put the stained spot under cold running water to dilute the stain, and cover it with enzyme laundry detergent. Brush the area with a soft-bristled brush (an old toothbrush, if you may) to ensure that the detergent works on the stain. Set it aside for about five to eight minutes before washing it as usual.

Ink

Put a scrap fabric or paper town underneath the stained spot. Spritz some hairspray on the stain and let it sit for a few seconds. Use a clean paper towel or cloth to blot away the excess ink. Redo the process until the ink stain is entirely gone, then wash the garment as usual.

Grease

Grease-fighting dishwashing liquid does wonders to any grease stain. First, rinse the stain by running cold water over the stain. Apply the dishwashing liquid and rub the spot to loosen the stain. Rinse and repeat the process if necessary.

Gently rub a laundry detergent (use a more powerful stain-fighting type if the grease is from motor oil) into a stain. Saturate the greased area with the soap, and let it sit for about ten minutes or longer. Without rinsing, run the garment in the washer with the hottest possible setting applicable for the garment.

Tomato

Put liquid detergent directly into the stain and rub it with your fingers. Rinse and repeat the process as many times as needed. If the stain lingers, apply an enzyme laundry detergent to the tomato stain and let it stand for about 20 minutes or more. Without rinsing the detergent, run the garment in the washer with the hottest possible setting the fabric can handle.

Mud

Allow the mud to dry and carefully scrape the excess off. Cover the stain with laundry detergent and add a little water. Rub the fabric until the soil is reduced. Rinse and redo the process until the stain is completely gone.

For colorfast fabrics, use a mixture of equal parts water and vinegar if the stain is not removed during the first attempt. Let it stand for a while and wash the garment with enzyme laundry detergent.

Tips in Ironing Clothes

The following recommendations will help you accomplish your ironing task without any hassle:

- Always follow label instructions (see ironing symbols and meanings above).
- Make sure that your ironing board is a well-padded one. If it doesn't have adequate padding, buy a board cover with padding. You can also add extra padding by placing an old but clean blanket.
- Use distilled water when steaming because it prolongs the life of your iron.
- When ironing in bulk, start with items that require lower temperature, then work your way to items that require a higher setting.
- You can eliminate stubborn wrinkles by misting the wrinkled part with water before ironing. A spray bottle works well to accomplish this.
- When hanging clothes, button up to the second button from the top to hold the dress, blouse, or shirt in place.
- Iron fragile, synthetic, and thick fabrics on the wrong side. Apply this method to your outfits with graphics to avoid melting the designs.
- Let the iron cool down for at least 30 minutes before storing it.

Folding Clothes

You will probably have a lot less space for your clothes than you had at home. Folding your clothes tidily will mean that they fit into less space than if they were just thrown in. You can get some handy gadgets to organize your clothing and save space, like shoe racks for the bottom of the closet, and clothes hangers that take more than one shirt.

There are many videos on social media showing great hacks for folding and rolling clothes to store them when space is limited. Maybe have a look.

Food

When you are living independently you have complete freedom in what you will eat. However, keep in mind that in every kind of freedom, there also comes responsibility. It's your responsibility to ensure that you stay healthy. It might be fun to eat pizza and donuts for the whole week, but it's not healthy.

College students have a limited budget, shared kitchen and busy schedules, making most meal plans look impractical and expensive. Ideally you would cook nutritious meals all of the time, but in practice that won't happen.

Food Hacks

Listed below are some healthy tips that will help you in your college life.

Choose Your Food Wisely

Eating healthy will look different for every college student, so it's necessary to find options that will work for you. As you make friends you'll also want to consider their food preferences, intolerances and maybe even allergies. You might need to consider the difference between vegetarians and vegans. Gluten and dairy intolerance - it's a long list. The most important thing to start with is to make a healthy meal plan that suits you.

You can still have tasty treats and the occasional junk food meal of course. But limit the chips and eat carrot batons instead. Have fruit to hand to eat when you crave something sweet, don't always turn to Oreos and cakes from the deli. Remember if you don't buy the sweet things you can't eat them, so avoid stocking up on them.

Keep a Three-Day Food Journal and Analyze It

Planning your meal is an excellent way to eat a healthy diet, even on a budget. For every meal, add two fruits or vegetables. For example, you might include banana, orange, or avocado in your breakfast.

You can use your food journal to create meal plans. Meal plans will not only help you to eat healthily, they will help you to save money. Instead of drifting around the food hall picking up items at random you will take what you know you need for the next few days.

For most college students it works to plan at least three days of healthy eating, followed by one 'free day,' when they can eat whatever they like. Then they follow another three day meal plan and so on.

Filling In Your Journal

Write down the list of foods you might want to eat or drink for three days. Once done, note how many portions you can eat from those. For example, if your appetite allows you to eat three ham sandwiches during breakfast, write three servings.

You can also write the list of condiments that you usually consume with your food, e.g., ketchup, mayonnaise, soy sauce, etc. Include notable condiments in your meal plans since you still need to buy them.

If you also eat fast food, kindly indicate how much you will eat their meals or how frequently you go to their chains to eat.

Write your daily activities, including workouts, travels, and mood. After all, our mood affects our eating habits since food is well-known to improve one's mood whenever we get stressed. Make sure to keep track of your activities as much as possible.

Food Delivery Orders

With the advent of technology, life is getting more convenient for everyone, including college girls, because of the growing trend in food delivery. It's easier now to order food online and have them delivered instead of dining out for a traditional meal.

USA Today recently revealed that 77% of millennials use a food delivery service. It is 26% more than all the diners in the United States (Sun, 2018). Because of the growing trend, apps like *Menufy* are now taking care of your food needs via online ordering. Here are some tips to consider for making your online food-ordering service a better experience.

Order Food Early

Plan when you don't intend to cook because of your hectic schedule. When you opt for online food delivery, make sure you order early, so it's ready when you're home. You might leave instructions to the driver to leave your delivery in a designated place.

Food ordered online can be unhealthy, but it doesn't have to be, there are plenty of healthy options available too.

Improve Your Diet

With free access to late-night food delivery and dining halls with buffets, it's no wonder that so many college students gain weight.

In their first year on campus, one in every four freshmen gained ten pounds or more, according to a study of their diets. Those who gained weight ate fewer fruits and vegetables and more fatty foods and slept less than those who didn't gain weight (Sun, 2018).

Poor eating is also linked to getting lower grades, getting sick more often, and feeling more tired. There is also a higher chance of depression, anxiety, irritability, trouble focusing, and trouble sleeping.

Fast food and unhealthy snacks don't give you the nutrition you need to do well in school. Having a healthy, balanced diet from a young age can help you do better in school and get you into a habit of healthy eating.

You probably learned about the primary food groups and the food pyramid when you were still a child. The iconic pyramid created in 1992 became a symbol of healthy eating. It was integrated into the school curriculum and widely used in elementary school cafeterias for more than 20 years.

But in 2014, the U.S. Department of Health got rid of the food pyramid and replaced it with a new picture called *MyPlate*. *MyPlate* shows how much of each of the five primary food groups you should eat instead of how many servings you should eat.

MyPlate says that fruits and vegetables should make up about half of your diet. It likewise tells people to eat less dairy and grains than the original food pyramid said they should.

Your Daily Calorie Requirements

In 1992, the USDA said that most adults should eat about 2,000 calories per day. But because of new research, the

USDA now says that most of us don't need 2,000 calories every day. Also, the department says we should eat more vegetables and fewer grains. People of different ages, sizes, and physical activity levels can have very different calorie and portion size needs. An NFL linebacker should eat about 3,500 calories on game day, but a college sophomore working on a term paper might only need half of that.

Even between the ages of 19 and 30, the recommended daily intake for men and women is nearly 20% different.

How Much of Each Food Group Should You Eat Every Day?

Knowing how each food group affects your body can determine what you should eat and how much. Let's go back to review what we had learned about nutrition and healthy eating.

Grains

Women should eat between 6 and 8 ounces of grains every day, while men should eat 8 to 10 ounces.

Whole grains and refined grains are the two types of grains that people can buy. Adding whole grains to our diets makes us less likely to have heart problems, and we need fibers to aid us in our digestion.

Whole grains make you feel fuller. You'll feel full faster and eat healthier than if you eat refined or enriched grains.

Protein

Women should eat 5–6.5 ounces of protein every day, while men should get between 6.5-7 ounces of protein daily.

Protein is an integral part of what makes up the human body. We need it to keep our muscles, bones, blood, skin, and joints healthy. Protein turns calories into energy in its most basic form.

It's essential to get protein from healthy sources. Unfortunately, many high-protein foods are also high in cholesterol and saturated fats or made from trans fats and other harmful ingredients. Choose lean or plant-based proteins whenever you can to protect your heart health.

You should eat between 45 and 55 grams, or about six ounces, of protein every day, depending on your body type. Since most Americans eat a lot more protein than they need, this amount may seem low at first.

Dairy

Women should drink three cups of milk every day, while men should drink three cups of milk every day.

Dairy's main benefit is calcium, which helps our bones and teeth stay healthy. Dairy products include anything with milk, but it's essential only to count dairy that keeps its calcium content. Even though cream cheese and butter are made from milk, they are not in this group. Dairy products are things like natural cheeses, yogurt, and milk in any form.

You should include low-fat or fat-free dairy in your daily diet. College students should eat about 3 cups of dairy every day. It might be as easy as drinking a couple of glasses of milk.

Fruits and Veggies

Fruits and veggies are women's best friends. Consume at least four to five cups of fruits and vegetables daily, while men should eat five to five and a half cups of fruit and vegetables every day.

Fruits and vegetables are full of good things for your body, such as potassium, fiber, vitamin C, and folate. They are also low caloric content and have no cholesterol, which is good for you if you wish to maintain a healthy weight.

You need fiber to help lower blood pressure and cholesterol, keep your bowels working well, and improve your heart health. Fiber-rich foods make us feel full. College students should try to eat about two and a half to three cups of vegetables and two cups of fruit every day. This is the same as 12 baby carrot sticks, a good-sized salad, and two small pieces of fruit.

Fruit and Veggie Subgroups

Some nutritionists divide this food group further into subgroups based on the color of the fruit or vegetable: red, orange, green, blue, or white. To improve your diet, try to eat something from each of these groups every day as plants with bright colors also contain a lot of vitamins. It's also beneficial to remember that raw fruits and vegetables have more bulk and fiber. Cooked vegetables can be just as healthy, but you'll need to eat more to reach your daily goal.

Reconsider Your Appliances

Because you don't have a full kitchen during your stay in college, you will need to consider what appliances are practical in your room. Examine your kitchen appliances and reconsider them. Morning smoothies can be made with a single-serving blender. A juicing sieve can be used to make cold-pressed juice. You can make fresh almond butter for breakfast using raw almonds and coconut oil.

You can make delicious hummus with garbanzo beans to serve with pita bread or fresh vegetables. Cauliflower mash also works well. Cook your cauliflower in the microwave using a microwave-friendly package. Blend in the cheese, seasonings, and a splash of milk. It's tasty and a great way to get some extra vegetables.

Most dorm rooms have a toaster, at least. It would make delicious toast, but it would also be ideal for warming *naan* for open-faced pizzas or filling pitas with hummus, veggies, and feta cheese. A plate of bruschetta is a tasty go-to quick dinner. Just make some topping using a few ingredients and serve it on whole-wheat toast.

Prepare Your Snacks

When studying late at night and getting hungry, try to avoid getting tempted to eat candy, chips, or treats from a vending machine. Unbuttered popcorn, fresh or dried fruit, pretzels, rice cakes, or whole wheat crackers are excellent options. Try raw vegetables with low-fat yogurt or cottage cheese dip if you have a fridge.

Limit Your Daily Caffeine Consumption

Can you limit your coffee time to just one cup per day? A glass of tea will suffice if you have a late-night studying ahead of you.

Caffeine is hard on your skin and can make you irritable if you sit for long periods. It can become addictive and cause cravings. Carry a more healthy alternative with you, such as a bottle of flavored water. Drink whenever you feel tired of your body to feel revitalized and alert.

Tips for Busy Students on How to Eat Well

The average college student is often short on time, under a lot of stress, and eating on the go. You might find it hard to break bad habits like skipping meals or going to fast food places. But eating well can make you feel better, help you deal with stress, and help you do better in school and sports. After all, it's easy to get started.

Nutrition Tips

Eat breakfast well. Studies prove that skipping breakfast makes it harder to do well in school. Suppose you don't have time to sit down and eat breakfast, grab a bagel, a piece of fruit, and a glass of juice. Most of these things are easy to store in your room in the dorm.

Eat lots of calcium-rich foods. Those in their early 20s need to build up their calcium stores to avoid osteoporosis later. If you don't like milk, try to eat a lot of low-fat yogurts, low-fat cheese, and green leafy vegetables.

Limit how much sugar you eat. Sugar gives you calories but not many other nutrients and it causes tooth decay. Use it in small amounts and think about using sweeteners instead.

Eat healthy rather than diet. Starvation and quick-fix diets don't work long term and can be harmful. If you feel that you need to lose weight start by cutting out the sweets, treats and alcohol and eating healthily. You might be surprised by the results. Add in some regular exercise and see how you feel in six months time, we're sure you'll feel better!

Go to the salad bar in the dining hall. Depending on your choice, the salad bar in the dining hall can help or hurt your diet. Raw and green leafy veggies plus fresh fruits are all good for you. But if you love to have a lot of creamy dressings, bacon bits, and mayonnaise with your salads, bear in mind that calorie and fat content may be the same or even higher than what you would eat in burgers and fries, so choose wisely.

Drink plenty of water. Human beings need at least eight glasses of water a day; if you work out hard, you may need even more. Keep a water bottle anywhere you go and keep it nearby when studying late at night.

Limit how much alcohol you drink. If you drink alcohol, remember it gives you calories but nothing else. About 100 calories are in a light beer, wine, or an ounce of liquor. There are also health risks associated with alcohol.

Have fun eating. Food is more than just fuel for our bodies, so take the time to enjoy and savor it.

Visit Your Doctor

To know if you have any nutritional deficiencies, get a check up with your healthcare provider. You may have your blood checked to determine your state of health. If you have any deficiencies in iron, B12, Vitamin C, etc., you may augment your nutrition through meal preparation or take food supplements to meet your nutritional requirements.

Shopping Tips

Staying healthy and being on track with their budget can be challenging for college students. However, there are tips to follow to make your college life more convenient, beneficial, and right on the budget.

Have a Plan

You can't go beyond your budget, so make sure you won't be overspending. The most practical way to do it is to have your meal plan for a week and tick off the items needed as you buy them.

Make a List

Based on your meal plan, list all the things you'll need to buy. It saves you time instead of roaming the supermarket looking for what to buy. It will avoid impulse buying of food that you don't need, which may be wasted because you can't eat it quickly enough.

Shop with a Calculator

Use a calculator or the calculator on your phone to keep a track of what you have spent while you shop. Depending on the supermarket you may be able to scan as you shop, which will also help you to keep track. When doing your shopping, it's best to buy foods in season for a better deal. If you want fresh fruits or veggies, it usually pays to buy them from the nearest farmers' market instead of a supermarket.

To avoid spending beyond your budget, never shop for food when hungry. You are most likely to choose unhealthy foods and pick up too much.

Purchase Cold Foods and Lean Proteins

When shopping, consider ways to make delicious salads that aren't limited to romaine lettuce and standard greens. Add beans to salads to add extra protein, some dried fruit, and various vegetables.

Do you need a quick snack? Make a black bean salsa and keep it in the fridge.

Raw almonds and other nuts are a delicious way to add crunch to your meal.

Purchase instant grains to microwave and add to salads for added bulk. *Farro*, barley, and even instant brown rice work well.

What to Always Have in the Kitchen

When you have the space, maybe when you are in a flat share, you can put together a store cupboard of essential items you need to keep for cooking.

Stocking your kitchen with the following pantry essentials will make your college life more of a delightful experience than eating in the cafeteria or ordering food online.

- Onions
- Lemons
- Rice
- Oats
- Garlic
- Ginger
- Salt
- Butter
- Oil
- Vinegar
- Soy sauce
- Oyster sauce
- Sugar
- Chocolate
- Baking soda
- Honey

- Lemon
- Sesame oil
- Vegetable oil
- Ketchup
- Balsamic vinegar
- Red wine vinegar
- Chicken and beef stock
- Marinara sauce
- Canned goods (diced tomatoes, beans, fruits, etc.)
- Pure vanilla extract
- Granulated sugar
- Confectioners sugar
- Cumin
- Basil
- Rosemary
- Thyme
- Smoked paprika
- Curry
- Dried oregano
- Kosher salt
- Cinnamon
- Red pepper flakes
- Nutmeg
- Ground pepper
- Pasta and noodles
- Mayonnaise
- Milk

Other than the necessary ingredients and pantry supplies that you may need for cooking, think about the equipment that you want in the kitchen. These will include equipment such as a mini-fridge, microwave, coffee maker, Brita water filter, cutlery, dinnerware, and glasses.

Batch Cooking Weekends

Even if you've always relied on your mom's (or dad's) homemade cooking, don't be intimidated by cooking for yourself at college. Make use of cookbooks and recipes from the Internet. Watch videos to learn cooking methods.

Maybe you can get some hints, tips and even some practice with Mom or Dad before you leave home.

If you have space, you can also save time and money by cooking meals in bulk and storing them in the freezer.

Fast Meals

When you go to college you're going to need to be able to cook. Even if the dining hall is a convenient choice, it won't be available forever, and let's face it, you'll likely get bored of the food on offer. After a hard day of studying, the last thing on your mind is preparing a complete supper, but there are lots of quick and easy meals you can make.

Fast meals can be really simple! For example, the microwave can be used to make an overeasy egg. Add some avocado mash to some toast for a delicious breakfast. Add an egg to a pasta dish or a pizza for extra protein. Spread a bit of tomato puree and cheese on naan or pita bread for a quick and easy pizza.

Have a set of measuring cups in the kitchen to avoid having to use scales. When you are following a recipe use only one unit of measure, don't mix cups with ounces or grams, it will spoil the proportions.

Here are just a few meal ideas designed to be easy to put together and not damage your bank balance.

Breakfasts

The microwave oven can be used to make a **quick over-easy egg**. Have this on toast, maybe add some mashed avocado, for a delicious breakfast.

Use the fridge to make overnight oats. Use single serve bowls, small glass jars like Kilner jars or similar. You will need basic rolled oats, yogurt and fresh or frozen fruit. Put a layer of oats in the bottom of the container, as much as you want to eat. Then add a good layer of yogurt, approximately twice the depth of the oats. Add a layer of fruit. Cover with a wrap and leave in the fridge overnight. In the morning you will have a delicious breakfast. You can change this recipe up by adding honey, using granola instead of oats, or using milk instead of yogurt (put enough milk in to just cover the oats).

Make breakfast smoothies. Choose your favorite fruit, grains and vegetables to create your own smoothies. Popular options include:

Green smoothie - banana, celery, broccoli, spinach, milk and a small amount of spirulina.

Fruit and honey smoothie - banana, milk, honey, mango and other soft fruit that you have in the cupboard.

Lunches and suppers

You might like your main meal at lunch time or at the end of the day, so these recipes will work whenever you eat them.

Simple Mac n Cheese. Take half a cup of water, half a cup of macaroni, a quarter cup of milk, and a pinch of salt and mix them together in a microwave-safe bowl. Microwave for 2 - 3 minutes. Stir in a quarter cup of shredded cheese, cheddar is best and microwave for another 30 seconds. Stir and leave to rest for a minute before eating. For variety try adding chives, cooked chopped bacon, cooked sausage or spring onions.

Pesto pasta. Use a jar of pesto and some shredded cheese. Cook the pasta in a pan. Drain off the butter and stir the pesto through to taste. Add the shredded cheese and some black pepper. Re-heat for 30 seconds by stirring in the pan or microwaving if it has lost some heat and enjoy.

Simple pasta salad. This makes two servings, so you can share it or save half for the next day. Take one can of tomatoes, two servings of cooked pasta, chopped cucumber, tomatoes, canned or defrosted sweetcorn, feta cheese and a teaspoon of mixed herbs. Put the tomatoes and herbs into a pan, mix together and simmer for 10 minutes. Mix in the cooked pasta then leave to cool. When it is cool add all of the other ingredients. This is a tasty salad on its own, but you could try it with canned tuna, ham, cooked sausage - whatever you like really.

These are just a few ideas to get you started. Don't be afraid to experiment, you'll soon have a set of quick and easy meals to cook for you and your friends.

Snacks

Most college students' poor eating habits stem from a lack of thinking and preparation. Prevent this by planning your grocery purchases ahead of time. If you think you'll be studying late at night, choose some healthy snack options to satisfy your craving for crunch.

Try mixing almonds into a bag of organic microwave popcorn. It will add a little something special and keep you going late into the night—snack on dried cranberries, nuts, and a small apple during the day. Keep carrot and cucumber batons and celery ready in the fridge for snacking. The crunch satisfies cravings without the need for chips or late night fast food deliveries.

If you can't avoid eating fast food, make a good choice. Choose pizza with half the cheese, a regular-sized roast beef sandwich, a baked potato, or a green salad with low-calorie dressing. As much as possible, cut back on French fries, fried chicken, and fish sandwiches high in fat.

Vending Machines

College students also have access to vending machines in the school. However, this machine of convenience contributes to the rising levels of obesity. These vending machines provide limited healthy foods aside from being expensive.

Reconsider Your Appliances

Consider the space available to you and consider which kitchen appliances will be practical for you to use. Morning smoothies can be made with a single-serving blender. A juicing sieve can be used to make cold-pressed juice. You can make fresh almond butter for breakfast using raw almonds and coconut oil.

You can make delicious hummus with garbanzo beans to serve with pita bread or fresh vegetables. Cauliflower mash also works well. Cook your cauliflower in the microwave using a steamable package. Blend in the cheese, seasonings, and a splash of milk. It's tasty and a great way to get some extra vegetables.

Most dorm rooms have a toaster. Of course it will make delicious toast, but it would also be ideal for warming naan for open-faced pizzas or warming pitas to be filled with hummus, veggies, and feta cheese.

Study & exams

Have you ever wondered how college students like you got through their college years without putting their social life, health, academic success, and finances at risk? There are fantastic college hacks that help other college students maximize their well-being and effectiveness. They were able to have good grades and enjoy their time- and so can you if you put them to practice.

Classroom Hacks

Are you earning a bachelor's, master or doctorate? Whatever degree that may be, the following hacks can give you the success that you want:

Managing Your Schedule

If you want to have adequate time management, organize!

Think about the time you'll save if you already have your books and notes organized and if you have reminders set up for appointments and deadlines.

Here are some basic ideas to help you with getting organized, you choose which will work best for you:

Start the Semester with a Planner

Write down all assignment deadlines, activities, classes, exams, etc., to see everything at a glance and be able to think ahead.

At the start of the week or on Sunday, review your schedule so you can know what's ahead. Plan and diarize your time effectively instead of trying to remember what you need to be doing and when. Use a paper diary, electronic planner, an app on your phone - whatever works for you.

Keep your study space clutter-free and organize your textbooks and notes according to subjects. It will enable you to quickly access everything you need.

Use a Calendar and Online Management Tools

Have a look at this app – **myHomework Student Planner** – a time management app for high school and university students. It provides you with a calendar so you can track your assignments, projects, exams, and other activities. It also features a widget that lets you sync your assignments and receive reminders when they are due to avoid being caught in a deadline. This app is free, but if you want to get away with ads, you can have it for about $5 a year.

If you can, schedule your classes continuously, it will be more efficient than having them scattered the whole day. This way, you can head home earlier instead of commuting between classes.

Online classes will be another practical tip if you have a hectic semester. Online classes may require the same study time as the in-seat classes. However, you can access your modules online at your convenience to use your time more effectively.

Plan Your Weekly Schedule Every Sunday

Going through the week without a plan can be stressful and you run the risk of forgetting to do something. Taking time to plan your week ahead will provide you with enough time and space to figure out how to fit everything in and avoid the last-minute rush. Sunday is a day when you should be able to find some quiet time for planning. Do this and avoid your school days becoming frantic.

Do not skip class

It's tempting to skip classes when you don't like your professor, or the subject, or maybe you want to hang out with someone. However, remember you are there to study and reach your goals. Going to college is a significant investment. The longer you stay there, the higher the cost.

The US News declared the average cost of tuition and fees for in-state public college students is $21,629 and $35,676 for a private college (Powell et al., 2021). Remember that you and/or your parents are paying for these classes. According to Student Loan Hero, more than half of the college students in the US took out educational loans to pay for college in 2020, averaging about $29,800 in total for the time they spent in college. The average graduate paid approximately $400 monthly to pay their loan debt (Student Loan Hero, 2022). The US News and World Report further state that it takes 21 years for an average recipient to pay off their entire student loan (Bidwell, 2014).

Where to Sit

It's good that in college, you have more freedom to choose where to sit in class. But think about how your choice could affect your academic performance?

If you sit in the first few rows you will get a good view and be able to hear the class easily. You're also less likely to be distracted by students who aren't taking things as seriously as you, as people are less likely to mess around when they are close to the watchful eye of the professor!

You will get to know who the students to avoid sitting near. People who might be disruptive in their attitude to lectures, or maybe fidgety in class, on their phone etc. Just avoid the distraction of being around them.

Take Fast Lecture Notes

Taking notes is essential, you need to capture the key points of lectures so that you can refer back to them when doing further study, and for revision.

The average lecturer speaks at approximately 120-180 words per minute, which is just too fast for most people to keep up with, either in writing or typing into a device. So, writing down every word is quite impossible. However, there are hacks you can apply to take notes faster than any student.

Summarize the Lecture

The key here is to write down only the main points made and significant ideas. By summarizing the information, you are taking a more simple and organized approach than merely trying to take down everything that comes out of the lecturer's mouth.

If you attempt to take almost verbatim notes you will find that you generally won't actually take in what is being said. If you are taking summary notes you will need to listen and understand the lecture as it happens.

Summary notes are brief but to the point.

Here are summarizing tips for you.

- As the lecturer introduces a new topic, use that as a heading in your notes.
- Consider using bullet points to note the key facts and ideas under each topic.

- Use phrases and keywords that mean something to you, rather than trying to record actual sentences.
- After the lecture, immediately review your notes and expand on anything that you need to, so that you will easily remember what it all means even months or years after.

Mind Mapping

Depending on your learning style, sometimes words aren't enough to record and remember what was said at a lecture. Some people are more visual, and if you are one of them, you can try a more creative approach to note-taking through mind mapping. This tool allows you to visualize the overall structure of a specific idea.

Mind mapping also allows you to connect ideas within that particular subject, and when you can quickly highlight essential ideas. There are mind-mapping tools available online if you need help, and free videos demonstrating the technique.

Using Symbols and Abbreviations

You are already aware of the most common symbols and abbreviations you can use in your note-taking. It's a matter of integrating them into your notes to speed things up. For example,

- Numbers (#)
- Information (info)
- And (&),
- At (@)
- Weight (wt), height (ht)
- For significant notes (*)

To enhance your skill, try to learn the universal abbreviations for some commonly used words.

Another way to speed up note-taking is to drop vowels from words. Your eyes will still be able to read the words if you only used consonants, especially when you have done this for a while. This is sometimes called speed writing. (Or wrtng!).

Use a Speech-to-Text App

Using a speech-to-text app may be the quickest and easiest way to take notes. Since you are not doing any hard work but turn it on to record your professor's lecture, you are getting a massive load of information and won't be missing anything. It can be beneficial to have a transcription as a text version of your lesson to go back to if you are revising and don't understand your notes

However bear in mind that if you are revising it will take a long time to read through the whole of a long lecture. So it's worth taking brief notes at the time, then having the full transcription to refer back to when you need more explanation of a key point.

Here's a guide on how to use voice typing as a transcription tool.

- Create a new Google Doc and select [tools]
- In the toolbar, select [voice typing].
- Click the link above the [microphone icon.] It will start the recording. Once you see the microphone turn red, it means it begins transcribing.

Regardless of what approach to note-taking you prefer, there is one that works perfectly for you. Exploring the different methods is also recommended; you don't need to stick to just one strategy. You can even combine different approaches to your advantage.

Share Lecture Notes

Two heads are better than one. Most of the time, there are points that you fail to pick up when taking down notes. So, it's a great idea to find the time to share and compare notes with a classmate. They might have picked up some significant points that you overlooked.

Choosing a Major

Don't choose something because it's sensible or because people expect you to do it. Choose something you love. Choose something you can be the best at. If you choose something that you're not that interested in or don't hugely enjoy you are unlikely to take that skill in adult life working life.

Changing Your College Major

Sometimes college students need to switch their major, for many different reasons. If this happens to you, make sure you do it only once, and it's final. You won't want to spend extended years in college because you kept changing your mind. Remember that every wrong decision means additional cost, time, and effort that you wouldn't want to waste.

So, if you finally decide to change a major, here are the following steps that you must follow:

- Decide on what major to shift to.
- Review the academic requirements.
- Speak to your academic advisor about your decision.
- Submit all required documents.

Avoid Cheating and Plagiarism

There are two dishonest acts that you absolutely must not do - these are CHEATING and PLAGIARISM.

Cheating always involves the use of unauthorized sources for answering the test. It may also involve lying and taking credit for something that isn't yours. Unauthorized sources could be using concealed notes, the internet, books, or looking at your classmate's answers. School authorities decide what is authorized and unauthorized, as is stated on your college prospectus.

Plagiarism is presenting another individual's concept, idea, research, or project as your own. It's a violation of someone's intellectual rights, violating the school policy, and is also considered a criminal offense. To avoid committing this crime, which is punishable by law, you need to acknowledge and attribute the work of others by citing references or citations. Plagiarism is not limited to resources taken from a book, report, website, or journal article. It also includes those previously submitted by other students, even years before.

To avoid committing plagiarism and cheating, always think of their consequences.

To make sure you do not plagarize follow these simple rules:

- Do your work and don't pay others to do it for you.
- Present your original ideas.
- Cite all your sources when presenting ideas that are not originally yours.
- Use quotes.
- Use a plagiarism detector like Copyscape, Turnitin, or Grammarly Plagiarism checker.
- When in doubt, ask your professor.

Don't cheat:

- Avoid temptation by preparing properly for tests, exams etc.
- Keep your belongings away from you – especially your mobile phones and other devices.
- Only look at your own paper and avoid looking at other students' work.
- Don't share notes or test papers. It is also cheating when you allow someone to copy from you.

Bear in mind that if you cheat, you are depriving yourself of getting the kinds of learning that you set out to achieve. You are in college because you want to provide yourself with all the skills and tools needed for success, and cheating deprives you of having access to them.

More Tips

Early to Bed and Early to Rise

In the whirlwind of college life it might feel as if you never get time just for yourself. However, think about how it would be to have just one more hour at your disposal. How do you do this? Simple, get up an hour earlier. This is one of the most simple and powerful life hacks we can suggest to you. It will mean that you need to have a reasonable bedtime. It might mean that you struggle to get up for the first week or so. Once you have this habit though, it really can change your life.

By having an extra hour at your disposal, you can do anything you want, like eat a proper breakfast, exercise, revise or read a book, maybe go for a walk. Early morning is a peaceful lovely time of day, so enjoy it.

Get the best out of your sleep. When you have rested well during the night, you'll be able to use your time effectively, and you can participate well in your classes. You'll also be able to participate well in your classes. Your mind will become more alert than when you sleep late.

It will be easier to fall asleep if you are prepared for the next day. Pack your bag with everything you will need (notes, books, etc). If you know you have a lot on and want to make sure you don't forget everything, take just five minutes to make a to-do list. It will set your mind at ease before you go to bed.

Choosing your outfit, having your chores done, washing your hair, and preparing your meals for the next day will all mean that you can make the best of that extra hour you're giving yourself.

Limit Distractions

Learn to identify things that distract you, because they are the greatest time suckers for college students like you. Dealing with them can save you a lot of time.

If you think hanging with your peers or your roommates causes you to minimize your focus on study and take frequent timeouts, do your schoolwork in the library instead of doing it at home.

If Netflix or social media distract you, use an app like Self-Control or Clear Lock to block and limit your time on those websites.

Once you limit or eliminate time-wasting distractions, you can get your work time and use your spare time for recreation.

Ask for Someone's Help

There may be some subjects or concepts that you find difficult. Don't waste time going over and over something that just escapes you. Use your time effectively by seeking assistance, then you can move on.

Join a study group. When you discuss things with others, you will find the answers more quickly than when you try to figure them out alone.

Sift Your Extra-Curricular Activities

It's part of college life to take part in social activities. Just make sure that they won't take too much of your time to lead you astray from your personal college goals and studies.

If you are interested and want to be involved in numerous activities, remember that you will need to manage your time and probably decide that you can't actually do all of them. Ensure that each meeting or activity won't be a hustle to your studies and goals.

Sift through your priority interests and ask yourself if these interests will be valuable for your future. If you think you have a jam-packed schedule for the current semester, you can always hold off joining that group until you have a less intense schedule for the next one. Don't try to fit them all in one semester.

Try out these small tips, see the huge impact they can bring, and expect productive outcomes.

Study Hacks and Habits

College study hacks are quite different from those methods you may have used in high school, in college you need to think differently and more independently. Here are some proven study habits and hacks to help improve your access to information and memory retention, thereby improving your work and exam performance.

Where to Start with Studying

There are some very simple things you can do to set yourself up for successful study throughout your time in college. These apply to all of the different study that you will take part in, be it attending a lecture, taking part in a study group or taking part in a debate:

Show up to class - This might sound obvious, but a lot of students get very casual about lectures. Lectures are an essential part of your college learning experience. In some cases your attendance can affect your grades.

Be on time - Be on time not just for lectures but for everything. Even fellow students will get fed up if they are constantly waiting for you to turn up for things, whether social or studying.

Be polite - As the saying goes, politeness costs nothing. If you are polite people will feel relaxed and happy to be around you. However, don't confuse being polite with being a doormat - if someone is being demanding or abusing your good nature you don't have to go along with them.

Be helpful - We all like a little help sometimes. It tends to be the case that if you help others then others will help you, which can't be a bad thing. Casually offering some help when someone seems to need it can strengthen existing friendships and start new ones.

Be enthusiastic - We're not saying that you need to jump up and down and agree that everything is wonderful, that would be a bit off-putting for those around you! We're suggesting that you start by viewing the world in a positive fashion. When you are presented with a new idea, maybe that you don't agree with, don't instantly jump to squash it and put it down.

Try to start by thinking about the positive aspects and recognising them, then put your less positive view over in a balanced fashion.

Be positive - Following on from being enthusiastic - you will face challenges along the way, but try to look for the positive in every situation. If the day ahead of you looks like hard work, acknowledge that to yourself. Then think about the positives - what will you be learning during the day, which people you like will you see, and even - how great will you feel when it's over?

Find a Convenient Place to Study

It pays to be consistent when studying, so make it a habit. Find a spot where you can feel comfortable studying. Make sure it is free of distractions and conducive to studying.

This place might be in your room, but it can be depressing to spend too much time in one place. You might find a quiet corner of the library to be just the place you need.

Treasure Hunting – The Answers are Out!

Bear in mind that the questions set in college work are designed to be a rehearsal for exams. They will be in the form of tests, quizzes, homework, practice exercises, and other student resources. Bear in mind that you were provided with these exercises for a reason. Just be resourceful and don't waste any opportunity to learn from these activities.

Avoid Getting Stressed

Many students fail in examinations not because they don't know the answers, but because they get mentally blocked. Because they are more anxious about the thought of failing, what they have put in their brain was locked away somewhere that they just couldn't access when they needed to. It's hard to keep cool when you can't stop thinking about your exams, especially when you're not confident that you will pass them. Take every opportunity to practise in tests and by using sample questions from previous exams.

Discover your learning style. There are four types of learning styles.

- Auditory – learning through hearing
- Visual – learning through visuals
- Kinesthetic – hands-on learning
- Read or Write – learning through writing notes and reading textbooks and other materials.

Finding what learning style is more suitable for you can make learning more productive. Most students use a combination of these learning styles, so it pays to find out the style that works for you.

Study in Company

Two brains are better than one, and sometimes more than two brains are even better! You don't have to go through this college journey on your own. As soon as you start to get to know people who are doing the same courses as you, think about how it might be to work alongside them. Before you approach anybody to see if they would like to buddy up make sure that you consider whether you have a similar approach to them. Do they attend lectures and concentrate? Do they turn their assignments in on time? Do their comments and questions make sense to you? Do you like being around them?

These are some of the advantages of studying in company:

- First and foremost, studying with one or more people is an opportunity to practice your skills with people. This is great preparation for the world of work.
- Studying can become boring. Having company helps to keep the subject alive - you will bring different ideas and viewpoints together.

- You can help each other out with notes. If you have missed something in a lecture, or didn't quite understand the point being made, your friends can probably help you out.
- Bringing together learning from more than one person will improve your understanding and have the result that you will learn faster.
- You will help to keep each other on track. When you're studying you surely already know that it's easy to become distracted or to put off the work by doing something completely different. Study buddies set targets and help each other to keep to them.
- It can expand your horizons - members of your study group may be able to introduce you to new resources and course materials. They may be able to suggest useful study techniques that will help you to be more productive.

Organize a Study Group

Studying in company is a powerful study strategy as it combines multiple individuals' various strengths and interests. You can have a live study group, have on-line meetings or learn through a shared Google Docs folder. If you're the first one to organize this group, then you have full control of the group. You can share study docs, set up meetings, and benefit from everyone's knowledge.

A great advantage is that you have more than one person to call on if you need help. If you're working late and struggling to understand a key point, hopefully one of the study group will also be awake to pick up your text message.

Find a Study Buddy

You might prefer to work with just one person, or feel a bit daunted working in a larger group. Or you may just be lucky enough to have one individual who you work well with in addition to working in a study group. It's fantastic to find someone you really get on with who complements the way you study and learn, who can become your partner as you work through a course.

How to Make Studying With Others Work

Don't be daunted if you find yourself in a study group or pairing up with a study buddy who seems to be really on the ball with the work, or to be very clever. We all have our strengths and you might well be underestimating yourself!

People are choosing to study with you for a reason, so have confidence in yourself.

Think about the skills you bring to the situation and use them to help the dynamic. If you're an organized individual you might be the one to set up the study group meetings and on-line activities and actually make them happen. If you have a systematic and efficient way of sharing course notes, share that with your friends who make it known that they struggle with that. You might be a prolific reader who finds it easy to read additional materials and absorb them. You can share your extra learning with your fellow students.

A word of warning

Be aware that there are students who will use study groups and study buddies as a way of avoiding hard work. If you gradually realize that someone you study with isn't pulling their weight it will be a difficult situation, but you need to deal with it. If you're constantly being asked for your course notes, or to share your latest assignment, it's time to politely distance yourself from that student.

When you are studying with others you should feel that you are all taking part as equals, not giving a free ride to anyone.

Cost effective on-line materials

Always bear in mind that you are not confined to using the materials presented to you as you work through your course. Most universities and colleges provide free on-line resources for their students. Some of these are freely available to the general public. Find out what is out there that might help you.

It's also worth having a look at sources of cheap on-line learning, for example Udemy, Udacity and Skillshare. Take the time to research these to see what is applicable to your learning.

Improve Your Memory

Making good lifestyle choices – limiting stress, eating a balanced diet, getting enough sleep, and having regular mental and physical exercises is the best way to improve your memory. You could also use brain-training games to keep your mind agile.

Consider learning the following science-back strategies to improve your memory recall.

Organize Your Notes

When studying, outline information that you need to recall. You can highlight and focus on the most important ideas with an organized, detailed outline.

You can easily recall information using the chunking method that breaks down a large amount of data into smaller logical units for easy understanding. For example, learning a foreign language, you can group words into functional groups like nouns, verbs, adjectives, occupations, etc.

Make Associations

Make associations by creating mental images of things you want to recall and connecting them with sounds, tastes, colors, or tastes. For example, you want to remember a person with the surname of Barker. You can associate this person with the word bark by associating them with the bark of a tree or the sound of a dog.

Use Visual Cues

Learning can be much easier with visual tools like concept maps, graphs, photos, and illustrations. These tools simplify information, making it easier to understand and recall when needed. Visual cues are also great for boosting spatial memory as research has discovered in research among patients with Alzheimer's Disease and Mild Cognitive Impairment.

Saying It Out Loud

If you want to remember a piece of information, say it aloud. One study disclosed speaking aloud and hearing yourself will help to get information into long-term memory. The same research likewise confirms that memory benefits from active involvement (*Reading Information Aloud to Yourself Improves Memory of Materials*, 2017).

All-Nighter Tips

When things get too busy or when cramming for an exam, it's common for college students to skip a night of sleep. However, it's not safe to always fall back on all-nighters to finish your work. Health experts say that you must avoid pulling all-nighters as much as possible because of the adverse effects of sleep deprivation on your physical and mental health.

Pulling an all-nighter can leave you feeling tired, dehydrated, and with skin that looks unhealthy the next day. You may also find it hard to focus and may take up to a few days before you can catch up with your lessons. By not allowing your body to rest and recharge, your immune system can be impaired (Bologna, 2020).

It's best to sleep for a few hours instead of staying awake. Try sleeping for about 90-110 minutes to complete at least one entire sleep cycle (Yetman, 2020). Although one sleep cycle may not be sustainable, it can help restore your mind and body and get through the next day feeling less miserable.

College Activities to Try

A large part of your learning in college involves out-of-classroom activities – socialization, extra-curricular activities, community services, sports activities, etc.

Try getting involved in various groups or communities where you share the same interests.

Health

When life is too demanding for busy college students, they often let their health fall by the wayside, letting their academic activities overshadow attention to health habits – both good and bad. Good nutrition and health practices connect directly to one's physical, mental, emotional, and overall well being.

Sleep

Adults 18-60 years old need to have seven or more hours of sleep every night, while those below 18 must have 8-10 hours of sleep in 24 hours. This recommendation came from the Centers for Disease Control and Prevention (CDC) (Wallis, 2020),

Most students work hard and play hard, making time to both study and socialize. As mentioned earlier, they might pull "all nighters" or stay up very late. They are likely to have a large workload from the subjects they are taking. Added to that many students also have part-time jobs. All of this takes its toll, leaving them with low energy and motivation levels.

Students who have a lack of sleep will usually find that it is hurting their grades and health. This means that they give less attention in class, they also tend to cram before the examinations. Then they work into the night or even all night to catch up... It becomes a vicious and exhausting cycle.

Sleep deprivation can contribute to and be caused by mental health issues. Research done by the National Alliance on Mental Illness reported that 44% of students experienced symptoms of depression. About 80% feel overwhelmed by academic responsibilities, while 50% struggle with anxiety. Poor sleep likewise increases your risk of mood problems, affecting your grades and jobs.

Another significant consequence to consider is that a student who is deprived of sleep may be dangerously drowsy when driving. A lack of sleep can be hazardous and may lead to a vehicular accident. A study by the AAA Foundation for Traffic Safety divulged that you are twice more likely to get into a car accident when you only have 6-7 hours of sleep than when you have a full eight-hour quality sleep (Tefft, 2016). When your brain is tired, your response time slows down.

The negative impact of unfulfilled sleep requirements outweighs the benefits of a few hours of studying.

Benefits of Sleep

Sleep has many amazing health benefits, affecting almost every tissue in your body. It affects stress, growth hormones, immune system, breathing, appetite, cardiovascular health, and blood pressure.

Students need to sleep about eight hours to boost their physical and mental conditions. Here are some benefits you may reap from having enough quality sleep.

- Boosts immune system and heart
- Helps prevent weight gain
- Regulates mood
- Increases productivity
- Increases physical performance
- Improves memory

Use some sleep tracking apps to ensure you have a night of quality sleep. Most of these trackers are a watch that works by monitoring your body movements as you sleep. It helps you determine how much time you spent awake and the time you were asleep. Some sleep tracking devices even look at your heart rate change while asleep. These tools measure how much time you spend in each sleep cycle.

Examples of Sleep Tracking Apps are:

- SleepScore
- Sleep++
- Sleep Cycle
- PrimeNap
- Pillow

Since sleep sometimes seems like a luxury you can't afford when you are in college, developing healthy habits will help you get the benefits of good quality sleep. Relaxing your body and mind after a busy day is essential to better sleep.

Here are sleeping habits before bedtime that you can develop to help ease insomnia and transition to rest while improving overall sleep quality.

Develop a healthy sleeping pattern. Early to bed and rise is the best way to have a healthy and vibrant life during your college days. Make a habit of establishing a sleeping and waking time. Once your body's circadian rhythm gets used to your established sleeping pattern, you will find it easier to sleep and wake up on a programmed sleep schedule.

Read books before bedtime. Reading can put you in the right headspace for a good night's sleep. Reading is vital to strengthening the mind. A strong cognitive function helps lower mental chatter and lets you drop into a peaceful state of relaxation.

Stay off the Phone and Social Media. Checking your social media, reading news, or sending emails before bedtime can keep you awake. The nighttime use of electronics can affect sleep via the stimulating effects of light from the digital screen. It can interfere with your circadian rhythm – the 24-hour body clock that controls sleep-wake processes. The screen light on your device stimulates parts of your brain, making you feel more alert at bedtime when you should be winding down to relax.

Listen to music. Listening to music provides a total brain workout. A study about music has shown that listening to music has the following benefits (*Keep Your Brain Young with Music*, 2022):

- Reduces anxiety, blood pressure, and pain
- Improves sleep quality, mood, mental alertness, and memory

Some find that listening to audiobooks helps them relax and drop off to sleep.

Meditate. Do you know meditation can help you improve memory, concentration, and learning? Meditation is proven by science to enhance physical; health and mental wellbeing. It likewise reconnects you with what is present and vital in your experience.

Meditation provides you with inner peace and can help you be more successful in all your endeavors in life. It can help you to study more efficiently, improve your recall during tests, and decrease anxiety during challenging situations.

Do a Few Low-Impact Exercises. Some simple yoga positions or low-impact exercises like stretching can ease pain and aid sleep.

A review of studies revealed a link between meditative movements (such as Yoga and Tai Chi) to an improved quality of sleep, which as we've discussed before, will give a better quality of life.

Another exercise that can positively impact your sleep is stretching, which helps focus your attention on your breath and body, not stressors. Awareness of your body aids in improving mindfulness, which again will promote better sleep.

Sticking to gentle stretches before bedtime offers potential physical benefits – helping relieve muscle tension and prevent sleep-disrupting muscle cramps.

Drinks to avoid after dinner. Avoid caffeine after dinner for the reason that it will keep you awake and alert. Many people use alcohol to aid their sleep issues. However, alcohol decreases sleep quality by increasing nighttime awakenings, making your night less restful.

Nicotine in cigarettes is a stimulant. It can keep you awake. It can also cause problems waking up and also brings you nightmares. If you are smoking, try not to smoke two hours before bedtime.

If you want a hot drink in the evening, milky drinks will help you to relax and fall asleep.

Naps

An after-lunch nap can help boost your dwindling energy levels, but don't nap for longer than an hour and never later than 2:00 to 3:00 p.m.

Sleep Problems

If you have sleep issues like insomnia even after following our tips, consider checking up with the school physician. You may have sleep problems because of an underlying issue. Common conditions often associated with sleep issues include (*How to Keep a Mental Health Journal*, 2022):

- Mental health issues
- Diabetes
- Musculoskeletal disorders
- Kidney disease
- Neurological disorders
- Thyroid disease
- Respiratory problems
- Heartburn
- Heart attack & heart failure
- Diabetes
- Blood pressure
- Stroke

Water

Benefits of Drinking Water

Water is your body's principal chemical component and makes up about 55% to 60% of your body (Water Science School, 2019). Water is one of the bare essentials in life that we all depend on for survival. All parts in our bodies - cells, tissues, and organs need water to work correctly. Waters keeps every system in your body functioning properly.

The Harvard TH Chan School of Public Health claims that water performs many essential functions (*The Importance of Hydration*, 2018):

- Aiding your digestion
- Lubricating and cushioning joints
- Transporting nutrients and oxygen to all cells across the body
- Flushing harmful organisms from your bladder
- Preventing constipation
- Regulating body temperature

- Protecting body tissues and organs
- Maintaining electrolyte or sodium balance in your body
- Regulating blood pressure

You risk dehydrating if you do not drink enough daily.

The U.S. National Academies of Sciences, Engineering, and Medicine suggested that an adequate fluid intake for women is about 11.5 cups or 2.7 liters a day. Such recommendations include water, beverages, and fluids from food. Only twenty percent of your daily fluid intake comes from food and eighty percent from drinks.

Dehydration warning signs could be:

- Confusion
- Dizziness
- Weakness or low energy
- Low blood pressure
- Dark-colored urine

Can you drink too much water if you have certain health conditions like kidney, liver, or heart disease? If you have significant health issues check with your doctor.

If you take medication that causes you to sweat more, such as nonsteroidal anti-inflammatory drugs (NSAIDs), opiate pain medications, or some antidepressants, drinking more water can work to your advantage, check this with your doctor.

Remember that it's not only water that can keep you hydrated. Beverages also contribute to your daily requirement for fluids. Avoid sugary drinks as they can cause inflammation (Harvard Health, 2021). You can also try some herbal teas. You might try ginseng tea for energy and chamomile tea for relaxation.

The best way to consume water is to drink it throughout the day and at each meal. Bear in mind that you need to drink more water before, during, and after workouts, at high altitudes, when you have a fever, and during hot and humid weather.

To check if you're drinking enough, you should rarely feel thirsty, and the color of your urine should be pale yellow to colorless.

Eyesight

As a student, take care of your eyes because they will be working as hard as you. Eye issues can develop without signs or symptoms so make sure that you get regular checkups with an optician. If you wear contact lenses, consider leaving them out for a day if your eyes are tired and dry. Always remove your eye makeup before going to bed.

Several studies indicate that digital devices are harmful to human health. Eighty-eight percent of Americans know that digital devices can adversely affect their vision, but they still spend seven or more hours per day in front of their screens (van Hise, 2017).

The average millennial spends nine hours daily on devices such as smartphones, tablets, LED monitors, and flat-screen TVs.

As a student you won't be able to avoid spending long hours using screens. Make sure that your workstation is set up properly and take regular breaks away from the screen. Even if you just raise your eyes from the screen every twenty minutes and focus on a corner of your room it will help.

Approximately 11 million Americans beyond 12 years old need vision correction (*Keep an Eye on Your Vision Health*, 2020).

Common causes include:

- Too much time spent on screens
- Glare from computer screens
- Reading and studying with poor lighting
- Lack of eye blinking
- Not enough sleep
- Poor sitting posture
- Too close to the computer screen
- Uncorrected vision issues
- Poor diet
- Sharing makeup
- Inadequate hygiene measures like rubbing eyes, infrequent hand washing
- Swimming or showering in contact lenses

To reduce eye strain, we suggest that you:

- Position your desktop monitor roughly an arm's length away from your eyes to minimize any distracting screen reflections - e.g., windows or any shiny objects.

- Give your eyes a restful break by looking at something 20 feet away for about 20 seconds. Do this every 20 minutes.
- Blink regularly. Focusing your eyesight on the screen makes you blink less, which causes your eyes to dry and become uncomfortable.
- Use protective glasses, such as blue light prevention glasses, when working on screen.

Posture

Rounded shoulders are usually caused by muscle imbalances, poor posture habits, and excessive focus on specific exercises.

Nevertheless, having rounded shoulders can be alleviated. When your muscles and joints are used to hunch forwards, they can be retrained to find the proper resting position.

To correct your bad posture, you must be aware of everyday habits that may affect your sitting, lying, or standing. Sometimes, treating this issue is very simple. Because college students spend much time sitting inside the classroom or in the dormitory studying, many suffer from symptoms including upper back pain and stiffness, muscle spasms, headache, localized shoulder pain, and trap pain because of bad posture. Here are tips to prevent these and avoid back issues later in life.

- Consider your chair and how you sit.
- Review the position of how you look at your cell phone or desktop computer
- Make sure you have a good mattress
- If you wake up with neck pain, try a different or remedial pillow
- Walk and listen to audio
- Consider learning Pilates exercises, Yoga, the Alexander Technique or at least taking part in active sports.

Toothache

It is crucial to look after your teeth, especially when you're away from home. A little care and attention can avoid any toothache and other teeth issues. Brush and floss your teeth regularly after every meal. As much as possible, avoid sugary foods, drinks and sweets that generate acid in the mouth that may cause problems. In case of gum issues such as ulcers, gargle with salt water. Have a checkup with the dentist twice a year.

Skincare

Because we are constantly exposed to various pollutants in our environments, it is a must to cleanse your skin regularly, whether you wear makeup or not. Here is a skincare routine to ensure that you maintain fresh-looking and vibrant skin regardless of how busy you are.

After hopping out of bed, cleanse your face with lukewarm water and facial soap or wash to remove excess oil and dead skins.

When you shower, cleanse your whole body and use skin exfoliating body salt from time to time to remove dead skin cells. This will leave your skin feeling happy and refreshed. Also, don't forget to wear flip-flops in communal showers to avoid verrucas.

In the morning, take Vitamin C and apply SPF lotion before going out to protect your skin from the harmful ultraviolet rays. In the evening, you might use a retinol. Retinol exfoliates and brightens skin tone. It also improves your skin's firmness and elasticity.

Colds, Coughs, and Being Sick

While no specific food can cure an illness, eating the right foods can help relieve symptoms and discomfort, making you feel better. Here are some of the foods to eat when you're sick.

Fresh Fruits

When you have cold and flu symptoms, make sure that you have a stock of fresh fruits. They are full of vitamins, minerals, and other nutrients that can help boost your immune system. You may choose to eat various fruits, but citrus fruits like lemon, oranges, and grapefruits are rich in Vitamin C, which can help strengthen your immune system and fight colds and flu.

Herbal Teas

Even when you're not sick, herbal teas are good for your body because of their many health benefits. They are a great idea when you have colds and flu as they help relieve symptoms of sore throat and upset stomach and keep you hydrated. Ginger and green tea have sound anti-inflammatory effects. Mint and chamomile teas are great to soothe an upset stomach. Turmeric teas are thought to have healing properties. You could add honey to your tea if you can't drink unsweetened tea, as honey is soothing when you have a cold.

Soup

A bowl of hot chicken soup is great for making you feel warm and relaxed and for relieving fever and other cold symptoms.

First-Aid Tips

Since you will be living far from home, having a first-aid kit is a must. Anything can happen anytime; the best thing you can do is be ready.

First-Aid Equipment

- Digital thermometer
- Medical gloves
- Instant ice packs
- Disposable masks
- Hand sanitizer
- Medical scissors
- Hydrogen Peroxide
- Adhesive bandages
- Disposable masks
- Antiseptic wipes
- Cotton balls

Medications

For Wounds and Sunburns:

- Sunburn relief cream or spray
- Antiseptic ointment

For Aches and Pains

- Ibuprofen
- Paracetamol or acetaminophen
- Kerouac

For Colds and Coughs

- Fever relievers
- Nasal spray and decongestants
- Cough and colds medications

For Allergy

- Anti-itch creams
- Antihistamine tablets

For Digestive Disorders

- Antacid
- Antidiarrheal medications

Menstruation

Don't forget to take care of yourself during your period. For some it's not a particularly difficult time but many suffer from painful dysmenorrhea, bloating and possibly migraines. You're used to this when you were at home of course, but probably you had support from your family. Now you need to remember to take care of yourself.

It might be helpful to keep a menstrual diary. This will help you to make sure that you have the physical things you need at the ready. It will also remind you to be ready to take migraine medication at the first sign of trouble.

Have painkillers ready in case you will need them. Avoid caffeine and sugar when you have cramps, they can make them worse.

If you need to stop and rest, go home and do just that. Sleep if you need to, stay hydrated, avoid screen use. Keep warm and hug a heat pack or hot water bottle if it helps. You know your own body. If you develop any new or worrying symptoms consult a doctor.

Exercise

When you're really busy doing all that college stuff, you might think that fitness in college is unrealistic. Of course, it's not true! If anything you need to be even stronger and fitter to keep up with your workload. Regular working out is good for you.

Exercise is commonly known as the best way to get physically strong, but a new study shows that it can also make you mentally stronger by making you feel better.

New research published in the Journal of Happiness Studies shows that even 10 minutes a week of physical activity can make you much more likely to feel happy (Zhang, 2018).

Countless studies have linked physical exercise and happiness. Researchers found that people who worked out for at least 30 minutes several days a week were about 30% more likely to say they were happy than those who worked out for less time. They also found that getting more exercise can make you much less likely to become depressed (Mejia, 2018).

There's still much to be done to find out if there is an ideal amount of exercise to make people happier. It's thought that physical activity could be used to prevent or treat mental disorders, it will be interesting to see if research is carried out in the future on that. It's clear that there is a link between physical activity and mental wellbeing.

Many of the most influential people today, like Richard Branson, Mark Zuckerberg, Oprah Winfrey, and Mark Cuban, say that being physically active has helped them become successful and happy.

In her book "Time Smart," Harvard professor Ashley Whillans said that putting more value on time than money will make you happier and improve your quality of life. In an interview, she claimed that research repeatedly shows that people who put time first are happier than people who put money first. It is partly because putting time first makes us feel we have more control over our everyday lives. She says you should fill your days with "time-abundant activities," or ones that are important to you.

When you are studying hard, it can be difficult to find time for other activities. Whillans coined the term "happiness dollars" to show how happier certain things can make you. Let's say you get a $10,000 raise, for example. It's suggested that a raise of $10,000 will make you happier by a certain amount, so that amount is the happiness dollar value of the raise. However, you can do other things that will make you just as happy. Doing a form of exercise that you enjoy might also have a value of happiness is also $10,000.

Whillans suggested that, for example, getting help with chores can make you $18,000 happier. Just think of that when you and your roommate are tidying up!. She also said that you could be $1,800 happier if you spent 30 minutes a day on what she calls "active leisure." It could be anything from working out to helping others.

Cardio and aerobic Exercises

Exercise can help you do better in school. During exam season, it's easy to put your health and fitness at the bottom of your list of things to do. But do you know that exercise has a lot of benefits that will help you with your schoolwork?

Think about these reasons why you should try to get some exercise every day:

Higher Levels of Energy

Experts have found a link between being physically healthy and doing well in school. It is because low-intensity exercise can give us a much-needed boost of energy, which is excellent when you have to study for a long time. Studies also show that exercise makes people more creative and gives them more mental energy. So, if you need ideas, a walk or jog might be all it takes to develop something extraordinary.

Better Memory

Research shows that when you work out, your brain releases proteins that can help improve your memory and make you smarter. This is because those proteins have a significant effect on the hippocampus, a part of the brain that helps us remember things. So, regardless of whether you're studying for an exam or listening to a lecture, you'll find it much easier to understand and remember what you learn if you work out regularly.

Better Concentration

Blood flows to the brain when you do anything that makes you work out hard. It makes your neurons fire up and helps cells grow, especially in the hippocampus. It also means that if you work out for just 20 minutes before your study time, you can improve your ability to focus and pay attention.

Improved mood

Doing some physical activity makes your brain and spinal cord produce more endorphins. Endorphins are famous "feel good" chemicals produced by your body. Endorphins will also make you feel less stressed, improving your brain's function in several ways. So, if you start to feel like you have too much on your plate, regular exercise will help to keep stress at bay and help you maintain a positive attitude.

Now that you know that exercise helps your brain in many ways, why not go for a walk, jog, or run?

10,000 Daily Steps

You may have heard that walking 10,000 steps a day is good for you, but do you know why?

In the last ten years, the number of people who track their steps has exploded. People run to see how fit they are or to compete with their friends. The current advice is to take 10,000 steps every day - but why?

Even though this "recommendation" wasn't based on science initially, science shows that 10,000 steps a day are a great goal.

If 10,000 steps seem like a lot, there's good news. You can start with less and still benefit more from walking. Managing only half of that amount is linked to a lower chance of dying young. It doesn't mean that getting more than 5,000 steps isn't better, but even a little more movement each week is good for you.

Research shows that the more active you are every day, even if it's just light activity, the better. Many American adults find walking 10,000 steps a day hard, but it is possible (Upham, 2019).

Health Benefits of Light Activities

Surprisingly, even small changes in how much you move during the day can have significant effects. A recent study showed that the risk of dying early drops by 17% if you don't sit for 30 minutes daily. It includes walking, yoga, skipping, stretching, etc. Exercise with higher intensity, of course, has more benefits and reduces the risk by 35%.

How to Get Started

If you have never tried tracking your steps before, start by keeping track of your regular daily steps for a week or two. Then give yourself a goal to move more than you usually do.

The most important thing about keeping track of your regular steps is to be mentally prepared for days when you don't reach your goal and days when you go above and beyond it. Getting to 10,000 steps can be a good goal, but if you get down on yourself when you miss that target, you might want to re-evaluate. Just go outside and move around more than you did yesterday.

What Does the Number Signify?

The idea that 10,000 is a magic number came from a Japanese marketing campaign in 1965. A Japanese health science professor had invented a pedometer and thought that if people walked 10,000 steps a day, they wouldn't get fat. The pedometer was called "Manpo-Kei," which means "10,000-step meter." Since then, the advice to take 10,000 steps has stuck, but obviously there are no guarantees that you won't get fat!

Getting Into Sports

College girls indulging in sports have higher levels of self-esteem and confidence. They also have a lower risk of depression. There could be a number of reasons for this, being part of a team is likely to boost self-esteem and confidence for example, but taking part in sport is generally good for wellbeing.

Mental Health

While you often concentrate on your academic performance, you overlook your mental health. A research study suggested that 50% of mental health issues are established by age 14 and 75% by 24 (Mental Health Organization, 2016).

There are many ways to consider improving your health.

Mindfulness

Mindfulness is an approach to mental wellbeing that focuses on being aware of our feelings, thoughts, environment and even our bodily sensations. This should be done in a nurturing and gentle state of mind. Mindfulness helps us to live in the present rather than dwelling on the past and re-hashing negative experiences or worrying about the future. It has a calming effect and uses techniques including guided imagery and different relaxation and breathing exercises to soothe your body and mind.

Mindfulness can help college students to cope with the many pressures of college by teaching them to focus on things that matter most. It creates awareness while assisting them in mastering their emotions and dealing more productively with their workloads.

Meditation

One of the most effective approaches to practicing mindfulness is meditation. It is about soothing your mind and senses, achieving calmness, and reaching a state of tranquility.

Meditation involves practicing deep breathing, focusing on a certain point in space or your mind, and chanting a mantra. You can find free meditation videos on-line where a speaker will talk you through guided meditation.

Journaling

Another way to cope with stress, anxiety, and depression in college is through journaling. You can also use journaling to improve your behavior and habits.

When you are ready to start journaling, pick a convenient time to write every day about anything you find significant that happens during that particular day. You may spend 10-15 minutes doing this. Writing your journal can help you process your emotions and work on your self-improvement goals.

To start the journal habit, follow these steps.

Decide if you want to use pen and paper or a digital journal tool.

- Assign a convenient time for you to write in your journal. Could it be before bedtime, after your lunch break, or as soon as you arrive home in the afternoon? You may not necessarily do it daily. You can do it if you only have the time or during weekends.
- When you write, don't worry about your grammar or vocabulary. Just concentrate on your thoughts and emotions. Remember that you are doing this to express yourself so you can find a way to improve yourself.
- If you're having a tough time, think about whether you are still able to record at least one positive thing that happened during the day. It might be as simple as enjoying your lunch or exchanging a few words with another student.

Put anything you like in your journal and use any format you like. Some write their journal as a letter, others as a novel or a list. Include things that interest you or make you reflect:

- Poem or song lyrics
- Anecdotes and jokes
- Quotes that catch your attention
- Drawings or images

Use your journal for reflection and as a reminder of the things in life you need to deal with. Some examples might be:

- Feelings of depression or loneliness.
- Spending more time doing something you enjoy.
- Getting a medical opinion on something that's bothering you, for example a mole that needs checking out.
- The people in your life. Are there some you would like to spend more time with? Are there others who bring you down that you might want to drift away from?
- Anything that regularly causes you stress and plan how to deal with it.
- Obstacles to your studies and how to overcome them.

Technology Hacks

Let's think about how you can look after the technology in your life, so that everything is working efficiently and is properly cared for.

You'll want to get the best out of your devices and one of the most simple ways to do this is to maximize the efficiency of battery use. These tips will help to extend the working life of your batteries and generally care for your devices so that they run as efficiently as possible.

- Turn down the light - Reduce screen brightness. If it is available on your device make sure that adaptive brightness is turned on. This means that the device will automatically adjust brightness depending on the light in the room.
- Reduce notifications - Consider turning off push notifications and only checking messages periodically. This will also reduce distractions. If you still want to use push mail make sure that they are only turned on from the apps you are interested in.
- Reduce the "timeout" period. Set the time for your screen to close after not being used to say two or three minutes.

- Keep your operating system up to date, either by allowing auto downloads or by checking regularly to see if there are downloads waiting. This will mean that you benefit from updates that improve the efficiency of your devices as soon as possible.

- You could consider turning off wireless features such as Bluetooth and Near-Field Communication (NFC) to save battery life. If you do this just be aware that some of your favorite apps might need them to keep working correctly. For example, NFC is used for mobile payments by Apple and Google. If you have limits on your data plan you will want to use wifi when you're at home.

- Use Power Saver Mode - If you're using a device and are worried that the battery is going to run out, switch to Power Saver Mode. Most devices do this automatically when the battery gets very low, but there is nothing to stop you doing it sooner. It will affect the screen display and may turn off some features, but could be useful if you're working away from a power supply.

- Beware of apps that use a lot of power - playing games, watching films, surfing the Internet, playing music - these will all drain your battery down.

- Carry a battery pack - Keep a fully charged battery pack (or power bank) with you so that you can charge up when there are no electric sockets available.

- Care for your tech - Keep your devices dry and cool. For example if you're going to the beach, cover your phone and keep it out of direct sunlight. Make sure that the vents for your laptop fan are clean. Be aware that placing it on a soft surface such as your bed might block the vents and cause it to overheat.
- Eating and drinking - Crumbs don't help keyboards. Spilled drinks kill laptops. Think about what you have around your devices.

Caring For Your Computer

Take care of your laptop or computer because it's going to work hard for you.

- Clean the keyboard regularly using a soft brush or cotton swab between the keys and appropriate cleaning spray on a soft cloth. (Not sprayed directly onto the keyboard). You can turn your keyboard or laptop upside down and tap it gently to remove crumbs and other debris, but don't shake it! Spray cans of air for removing dust are great for cleaning keyboards.
- Clean the screen regularly with screen wipes.
- As in the previous section, pay attention to your battery use, close apps that are not in use, consider screen saver timing and energy saver options available.
- If you have to spend a long period of time working without access to power, put your laptop into Airplane Mode to extend the battery life.
- Consider having a spare battery for your laptop.

- Keep drinks well away from your computer. You might think you'll never accidentally knock your juice into your computer... until you do!
- Backup your data. Make sure that all your work is automatically being stored in the Cloud, or if you don't trust the Cloud an external device.Think about how much work you can do when you're busy, even in just thirty minutes. You would not want to lose it in a computer crash.

Google Chrome

Ways to Use Google in Searching Information

Google search is used every day by millions of people for a wide range of reasons. Students use it for school activities, people in business use it for research, and many others use it for fun. However most people may not be getting the most out of Google Search.

Want to use Google search more effectively and quickly find what you're looking for? Listed below are 11 tips and tricks to help you get the most out of your Google search:

Google tabs. Use the tabs in Google search. You can find multiple tabs at the top of every search. Most of the time, there will be web, images, news, and more. Using these tabs, you can tell what kind of search you need to do. Use the News tab to find the most recent news stories. You can also search by an image by dragging an image into the image section.

Detailed search hack #1 - Use quotes. Use quotes when looking for something specific to make Google search on point as much as possible. When you enclose your search parameters in quotes, you tell the search engine to look for the whole phrase.

If you search for Puppy Dog Sweaters without quotes, the engine will look for content with those three words in any order.

But searching for "Puppy Dog Sweaters" will only look for that exact phrase. It can help you find specific information that might be buried under other content if it isn't organized well.

Detailed search hack #2 - Use a hyphen to leave out words. You might sometimes be looking for a word with more than one meaning. Mustang is one such car. When you type "Mustang" into Google, you might get results for both the Ford car and the horse. If you want to filter one, use a hyphen to tell the engine not to look at the other.

Typing "Mustang-cars" tells the search engine to look for mustangs but to get rid of any results that include the word "car." It can be helpful when you want to find out about something without learning about something else.

Sites that are like other sites. Let's say you have a website you like to visit, but it is starting to get boring, and you want to find more like it. It is a trick you can use.

By typing "related:amazon.com," you will find links to online stores like Amazon. Online stores like Barnes & Noble, Best Buy, and others sell physical goods. It's a powerful Google search tool that can help you find new sites to look at.

Math with Google Search. Google Search can help you with math. You can ask Google basic questions or some more difficult ones. It's important to remember that Google won't solve all math problems but will solve a good number of them.

In the Google search bar type in: 5*5=

Then google will show you the answer.

Look for more than one word at once. Google search is easy to change. It knows that you might not find what you're looking for if you only search for one word or phrase. So, it lets you look for more than one.

You can search for one word or phrase along with another word or phrase by using this trick. It can help you narrow your search to find what you want.t

You can find both phrases by typing "How to Prepare for a Job Interview the Best Way" OR "What to Do to Get Ready for a Job Interview." Although the parameter is the same as the quotes, only these two phrases will be searched for.

It can also be done with words, for example, by typing "white chocolate OR chocolate" without the quotes. It will look for pages that have either chocolate or white chocolate!

Shortcuts on Google Search. You can type in many commands that will give you results right away.

Like the math example above, Google can immediately give you the necessary information. It will be at the top of the search results. It can save you time and effort by keeping you from having to click on many annoying links.

Here are some of what you can tell Google to do:

- Weather *zip code* – This will tell you what the weather is like in the given zip code. You can also use the names of towns and cities instead of area codes, but this may not be as accurate if the city has more than one area code.

- What is (name of celebrity) 's Number? It is a fun little thing that will tell you how many connections any celebrity has to the famous actor Kevin Bacon. Six Degrees joke of Kevin Bacon is a popular joke that says no actor is more than six links away from Kevin Bacon. The Bacon Number for Mark Zuckerberg is 3.

Another example of math is the one shown above.

- What does the word "word" mean? Or Define *word*: This will show you what a word means.
- Time *place*: If you type in a location, this will show the time there.

You can check any stock by going to Google and typing in its ticker name. If you search for GOOG, the stock prices for Google will be checked.

With these quick commands, a web search that usually takes several clicks can be done in just one. It is beneficial if you need the same information over and over.

Specific file types. People often forget that Google search lets you look for a particular file or type. It can be very useful if you need to find a PDF or PowerPoint file you saw before or used for another project. It's easy to understand:

filetype:pdf *Search term here*

In the example above, you must change the search term to whatever you're looking for. Then, use the filetype command and enter the extension for any file type you can think of.

It is primarily useful for academic purposes but can also be helpful for business and other types of presentations.

Changes in money and units. When searching via Google, you can quickly and accurately convert both units of measure and the value of a currency. You may use it for many things, such as checking the exchange rate between two currencies. If you are learning math, you can use it to change feet to meters or ounces to liters. Here's what you need to do:

Miles to km: This will change miles to kilometers. You can change a number by putting a number in front of it. Like, "10 miles to km" will tell you how many kilometers are in 10 miles.

US Dollars to British Pounds: This turns one US dollar into one British pound. Like the measurements above, you can add numbers to find exact conversions for a certain amount of money.

This tip is indeed for math students and people who do business worldwide. But you'd be surprised at how often regular people use these tips.

Follow up on your Packages. The last thing you can do to find your packages is to use Google. You can put the tracking number for any UPS, USPS, or FedEx package right into the Google search bar, which will show you where your package is.

It's much easier to do this than to go to each site, wait for it to load, and then look for your packages. Just type in your package's tracking number to find out where it is.

Google Search is a very effective way to find information. You can find anything you need on the World Wide Web using the tips above. There is a way to make it work for you, whether you need to avoid Wikipedia for a school essay project, find the latest stock prices, or look up song lyrics.

Creating Folders on the Google Chrome Top Bar

To make a folder: If you have multiple bookmarks on the same subject on your Chrome browser, you might want to make a folder to keep them all in one place. First let's make a few folders on your google chrome top bar. I would suggest you start with these folders College, Trips, Family, Social media, etc. Here is how you make a folder on Google Chrome.

Right click on your Google Chrome browser.

Click ADD FOLDER.

Name your new folder and click SAVE.

Then you bookmark a webpage (maybe it's a trip you're planning, or an online study resource you need for college), it will appear on the google chrome top bar. Drag this name to one of the new folders you created.

Money

You're young, you're free and you're at college. It may feel like the world's your oyster, but of course there are limits. One of those is that you will need money to get out and socialize, go to gigs and generally have fun. To make sure you make the best of your money, so that you have enough for essentials as well as some treats, you will need to learn to manage your finances.

Being at college you have a great opportunity to develop good money management. This will help you to avoid financial stress and also help you to develop habits that will help you for the rest of your life.

You should use this time to calculate exactly how much money you need on a weekly basis as you go through college. Then you will know how much money you will have available to start saving. Doing this will mean that you can start to think about future goals, such as traveling, paying off your student loan and other milestones such as finding your own place when you leave college.

Managing Your Money

Let's think about some key skills that you will need to develop to manage your money. These will include setting a budget, monitoring your expenditure, saving and managing debt. These skills are as important as the skills you will be developing to support you in your studies. Also if you feel confident about your money management you will not be worried about making ends meet, or distracted from your studies by that worry.

Aim to embark on college life in good financial shape and be in the same great situation when you graduate.

Budgeting and tracking expenses

Mapping your budget and setting your financial goals may seem overwhelming after having a long day of class activities, lessons, etc. (not to mention your other obligations outside school). However, setting up a budget plan could also be not as tough as you think.

You will need to consider three significant budgeting elements:

- Earnings
- Expenses
- Savings

Tracking all these three, either manually or using a budget app, will help you manage your monthly budget.

Creating your monthly budget plan and tracking your habitual spending will give you an insight into where your money goes. You will be able to see if you set your budget correctly and if not, re-assess the plan. Be prepared to cut back if you find you are spending too much on any area, but don't set a plan that is too tough to stick to. You are allowed to have some treats and you will deserve a break from your college work.

Now, think about everything that needs to be paid monthly or prioritized, such as:

- Basic college expenses like tuition, room, and board (if you are living outside campus)
- Textbooks and class supplies
- Car insurance and payments or transportation costs
- Haircut

- Toiletries
- Food
- Phone

Use a spreadsheet or use a budget planning tool or app to set up your budget plan. Enter each of your items of expenditure into the plan with a realistic estimate of what it will cost each month. Total it up and you will know if your spending plans are realistic and manageable.

Set up another spreadsheet to use for recording what you actually spend during the month. Note how much you spent and what it was spent on. This may seem like a tiresome exercise, and it would be easy to forget to do it. However if you take the time it will be really useful to be able to compare this to your original budget plan to make sure that your original estimates were on track.

There are tracking apps, such as Wall, Acorn or Mint, that you can use to make monitoring your budget easy.

What will you do with any money left over? The sensible thing would be to save it for unexpected expenses in the future. We're sure that sometimes you'll instead use it for a fun night out with friends!

Savings

Many people struggle to save. It's so easy to just spend all of our money and forget about the future. If you can set up good saving habits when you are young then saving becomes easy. It is usually something that people will continue to do for the rest of their lives.

The easiest way to save is to include an amount to be saved each month in your budget plan. Then, rather than transferring money each month, set up a standing order for the money to be moved automatically each month. After a few months you will almost forget that it's happening.

A savings pot will be a great help when unexpected expenses come up. Maybe you'll need a particular book, or your laptop will need repairing, or there will be a field trip you want to go on. Having savings will help you to avoid using credit for these expenses.

Your savings will be your emergency fund, something everyone would like to have.

How to keep expenses down

Plan Your Meals. As we've mentioned earlier in this book, planning your meals so that you can avoid impulse buying in the supermarket is a great way to control spending. Avoid pricey takeouts or eating out. If you and your roomie get on well you might be able to meal plan and shop together, which could save even more.

Save on textbooks and devices. Rather than purchasing new editions, rent or buy old textbooks. Other, less expensive coursework resources may be available through your college.

If you need new technology for class, consider buying a refurbished model rather than a new one.

Instead of spending much on fuel, insurance, and parking space fees throughout your college years, why not consider walking, riding your bike, or taking public transportation?

Budgeting and saving, like so many other aspects of life, require time and experience to master. Don't be concerned if you occasionally make errors or go over budget. Just tweak your budget plan and get back on track. Maintain your focus on developing sound financial habits and you won't regret it.

Making Money

Even while you are in college, there are many ways you can make money. You can work part-time, have summer jobs, or work online as a freelancer. Online platforms offer various gigs and side hustles, allowing you to work during the available time. Here are some of them.

- Upwork
- Freelancer
- Fiverr
- TopTotal

There are unlimited ways to earn money physically or virtually. It's just a matter of finding what is best for you and tapping into these resources.

Gaining job experience now will help you after college when seeking employment. You will start to learn about the world of work. Earning your own money will help to boost your confidence and self-esteem and give you more independence. You might be able to pay money towards your tuition, meaning that you will need to borrow less in the future.

When you start job hunting you could consider looking for opportunities to use skills that you already have. On the other hand, it could be an opportunity to be trained in something completely new.

If you only want to work during the summer, make the most of your summer employment. Consider taking on additional shifts to make extra money to save. You might also consider doing an internship, which would provide you with both money and real-world experience if it is paid.

Success does not happen overnight, so if the going is a bit tough at first don't give up. Earning money during your time at college can mean that your life is a bit more comfortable there. It may mean that you have some cash in hand after graduation. It might even give you a healthy bank balance to give you a solid financial foundation for your future.

Avoiding Debt

Credit cards can provide convenient access to items for things you need, but also those you don't need. They are a temptation to spend money even when you don't have any. To buy that nice item of clothing or tech gadget now, rather than in a few weeks when you've saved up. In short, credit cards are a great way to drown yourself in debt quickly.

Avoid getting yourself into debt. This may seem obvious now but you might need to keep reminding yourself when you are in college. Think of ways to support yourself financially so that you don't feel so tempted. We've talked about working in college, you could also consider applying for scholarships and grants. Every college and university makes grants, with the number one eligibility requirement being high school grades.

Student Loans

Student loans have become a serious issue for students, not only in the United States. US Student loan totals have reached over $1.73 trillion (Hess, 2021). UK graduates have the highest student loan debt in the developed world. The average student will accrue over 50,000 pounds of debt before graduation (University of the People, 2022).

With such statistics, the best way to avoid debt is by earning income and paying for your education, with or without your parents' support. If this may sound impossible in your case, paying for a part of your loan while still in college can make a huge difference. The sooner you can earn money to finance your schooling, the less dependent you are on an educational loan.

If you intend to apply for a student loan, try not to take a loan amount higher than your expected first year's salary. It's best to choose federal loans over private loans because the government offers fixed interest rates. Also, learn about the deferment period to determine when you should pay back or if there is a chance for loan forgiveness.

Plan Ahead for Debt Pay Off

Two out of every three 2018 graduates had student debt, according to The Institute for College Access and Success. After your grace period expires you'll have to repay your student loans. Going from paying nothing to hundreds of dollars per month may seem surreal. You may design a long-term debt payoff plan that sets you in a good position once you graduate if you consider your total expected debt, repayment schedules, and interest.

If you've accumulated a lot of student loans, personal loans, or credit card debt you'll need a strategy to repay them.

It would be best to confront your debt head-on as soon as possible to build a stable financial future. You can pay off the debt using different methods, but the one that keeps you motivated is the best option. For example, set your monthly payment plan with some small rewards along the way. Plan that when you have paid the first 12 months of payments without missing a month you can get yourself a reward, maybe a concert ticket or an item of clothing you'll love.

Start Investing

The earlier you invest, the longer the time your money will earn interest and the more money will be in your pot for when you need it. Think about setting up a personal pension plan as soon as you start work, the earlier you start the larger your pension will be.

Investing is much easier than you would believe. You can start an account online with a little deposit and set up automatic monthly transfers to your investing account from your bank account. If you're considering starting an Individual Retirement Account or investing in the S&P 500 or similar, do your homework beforehand and consider getting independent financial advice.

Test Out Financial Planning Apps and Resources

Aside from your bank's app, there's much more to managing money on your phone. Nowadays, budgeting services such as Mint and You Need a Budget can help you organize your finances in ways that make saving easier.

Experiment with a few to see how they perform. They may not be the ones you want to use in the long run, but knowing how each program works will help you sort through various money management approaches to discover the one that's right for you.

Your work is never done when it comes to financial literacy. Like everything else in life, the money world is constantly changing and rebranding.

You may believe that the tools and knowledge you've acquired are ample at this time, but you never know what financial problems and opportunities lie ahead of you.

Search for and follow a reputable media outlet (such as Forbes, Bloomberg, The Balance, or The Motley Fool) on social media platforms or subscribe to their newsletters if you trust their advice.

Finally

What more can we say? We hope that this book has given you some help and ideas as you prepare for this next huge and exciting step in your life. From living away from home to managing your money, from keeping healthy to the world of dating, we've tried to share the things that we wish we'd been told before we embarked on college life.

Please don't be daunted by the prospect of going to college. Yes, it might be a bit challenging at times, you might feel out of your depth at first, but you've got this! Your time at college is going to be amazing. You will meet fascinating people and make great friends, some of whom will be friends for life. You will go into college as a child and leave an adult ready to make your way in the world. And your college days will be the best days of your life.

Enjoy the journey!

And one last note… before you go, I have a small request to make. I would really appreciate it if you could review this book and share your lessons learned. Doing so will help me a lot in getting this book out to other young adults who can benefit from the college tips and strategies I have shared. Thank you.

Enjoy the next book in this series:

Adulting for Beginners

Life Skills for Adult Children, Teens, High School and College Students

MATILDA WALSH

References

Bidwell, A. (2014, October 7). *Student Loan Expectations: Myth vs. Reality*. US News. https://www.usnews.com/news/blogs/data-mine/2014/10/07/student-loan-expectations-myth-vs-reality

Bologna, C. (2020, February 20). *The Scary Ways An All-Nighter Messes With Your Body And Brain*. HuffPost. https://www.huffpost.com/entry/what-happens-when-you-pull-an-all-nighter_l_5dd5b559e4b010f3f1d21d30

Freshman 15: College Weight Gain Is Real. (2009, July 28). WebMD. https://www.webmd.com/diet/news/20090728/freshman-15-college-weight-gain-is-real#:%7E:text=A%20new%20study%20shows%20that,pounds%2C%20during%20their%20first%20semester.

Harvard Health. (2021, April 12). *Playing with the fire of inflammation*. https://www.health.harvard.edu/staying-healthy/playing-with-the-fire-of-inflammation

Hess, A. J. (2021, September 9). *The U.S. has a record-breaking $1.73 trillion in student debt—borrowers from these states owe the most on average*. CNBC.

https://www.cnbc.com/2021/09/09/america-has-1point73-trillion-in-student-debtborrowers-from-these-states-owe-the-most.html

How to keep a mental health journal. (2022, May 11). MHA Screening. https://screening.mhanational.org/content/how-keep-mental-health-journal/?layout=actions_ah_articles,light

The importance of hydration. (2018, June 22). News. https://www.hsph.harvard.edu/news/hsph-in-the-news/the-importance-of-hydration/

Keep an Eye on Your Vision Health. (2020, October 1). Centers for Disease Control and Prevention. https://www.cdc.gov/visionhealth/resources/features/keep-eye-on-vision-health.html#:%7E:text=Improving%20your%20eyesight%20is%20important,early%20and%20preserving%20your%20vision.

Keep Your Brain Young with Music. (2022, April 13). Johns Hopkins Medicine. https://www.hopkinsmedicine.org/health/wellness-and-prevention/keep-your-brain-young-with-music

Mejia, Z. (2018, May 3). *Just 10 minutes of exercise a week can make you significantly happier.* CNBC. https://www.cnbc.com/2018/05/03/just-10-minutes-of-exercise-a-week-can-significantly-make-you-happier.html#:%7E:text=Generally%2C%20the%20type%20of%20exercise,in%20less%20time%2C%20researchers%20found.

Mental Health Organization. (2016, June 7). *Mental health statistics: children and young people.* Mental Health Foundation. https://www.mentalhealth.org.uk/statistics/mental-health-statistics-children-and-young-people

Nair, M. (2022, February 23). *How to Avoid Student Loan Debt? Useful Tips!* University of the People. https://www.uopeople.edu/blog/how-to-avoid-student-loan-debt/

Powell, F., Kerr, E., & Wood, S. (2021, September 17). *What You Need to Know About College Tuition Costs.* US News. https://www.usnews.com/education/best-colleges/paying-for-college/articles/what-you-need-to-know-about-college-tuition-costs

Reading information aloud to yourself improves memory of materials. (2017, December 1). ScienceDaily. Retrieved June 27, 2022, from https://www.sciencedaily.com/releases/2017/12/171201090940.htm

Student Loan Hero. (2022, April 6). *A Look at the Shocking Student Loan Debt Statistics for 2022.* https://studentloanhero.com/student-loan-debt-statistics/

Sun, L. U. T. (2018, October 13). *Online food delivery market could grow to $24B by 2023: A Foolish Take.* The Motley Fool. https://eu.usatoday.com/story/money/food/2018/10/13/online-food-delivery-grubhub-ubereats/38089847/

Tefft, B. (2016, December). *Acute Sleep Deprivation and Risk of Motor Vehicle Crash Involvement*. Foundation for Traffic Safety. http://publicaffairsresources.aaa.biz/wp-content/uploads/2016/11/Acute-Sleep-Deprivation-and-Risk-of-Motor-Vehicle-Crash-Involvement.pdf

University of the People. (2022). *How to Avoid Student Loan Debt? Useful Tips!* https://www.uopeople.edu/blog/how-to-avoid-student loan-debt/

Upham, B. (2019, September 25). *Large Study: Low-Intensity Activity Has Health Benefits*. EverydayHealth.Com. https://www.everydayhealth.com/fitness/large-study-light-intensity-activity-health-benefits/

van Hise, K. (2017, March 13). *Put Your Digital Devices to Bed Early: Optometrists Caution Overexposure to Blue Light May Cause Health Issues|EyeCare.org*. Eye Care Organization. https://eyecare.org/site/put-your-digital-devices-to-bed-early-optometrists-caution-overexposure-to-blue-light-may-cause-health-issues/#:%7E:text=The%20American%20Optometric%20Associatio n's%20(AOA,day%20looking%20at%20their%20screens.

Wallis, A. (2020, June 24). *How Much Sleep Should a College Student Get?* Southern New Hampshire University. https://www.snhu.edu/about-us/newsroom/education/how-much-sleep-do-college-students-need#:%7E:text=well%20in%20school.-,According%20to%20the%20Centers%20for%20Disease%20Control%20and%20Prevention%20(CDC,in%20a%2024%2Dhour%20period.

Water Science School. (2019, October 22). *The Water in You: Water and the Human Body | U.S. Geological Survey*. USGS: Science for a Changing World. https://www.usgs.gov/special-topics/water-science-school/science/water-you-water-and-human-body#:%7E:text=In%20adult%20men%2C%20about%2060,their%20bodies%20made%20of%20water.

Yetman, D. (2020, October 8). *Is It Better to Sleep for 1 to 2 Hours, or to Not Sleep at All?* Healthline. https://www.healthline.com/health/is-2-hours-of-sleep-better-than-no-sleep#summary

Zhang, Z. (2018, March 24). *A Systematic Review of the Relationship Between Physical Activity and Happiness.* SpringerLink. https://link.springer.com/article/10.1007/s10902-018-9976-0?error=cookies_not_supported&code=c1fa2959-e7b0-4d7a-b01d-bbffe09d03cb

Made in the USA
Las Vegas, NV
18 February 2023

67755208R00105